Alma Mahler and Her Contemporaries

ROUTLEDGE MUSIC BIBLIOGRAPHIES

RECENT TITLES

COMPOSERS

Isaac Albéniz, 2nd Edition (2015)
Walter A. Clark

William Alwyn (2013)
John C. Dressler

Samuel Barber, 2nd Edition (2012)
Wayne C. Wentzel

Béla Bartók, 3rd Edition (2011)
Elliott Antokoletz and Paolo Susanni

Vincenzo Bellini, 2nd Edition (2009)
Stephen A. Willier

Alban Berg, 2nd Edition (2009)
Bryan R. Simms

Leonard Bernstein, 2nd Edition (2015)
Paul R. Laird and Hsun Lin

Johannes Brahms, 2nd Edition (2011)
Heather Platt

William Byrd, 3rd Edition (2012)
Richard Turbet

Frédéric Chopin, 2nd Edition (2015)
William Smialek and Maja Trochimczyk

Miles Davis (2017)
Clarence Henry

Frederick Delius, 2nd Edition (2009)
Mary Christison Huismann

Gaetano Donizetti, 2nd Edition (2009)
James P. Cassaro

Edward Elgar, 2nd Edition (2013)
Christopher Kent

Gabriel Fauré, 2nd Edition (2011)
Edward R. Phillips

Alberto Ginastera (2011)
Deborah Schwartz-Kates

Fanny Hensel (2018)
Laura K.T. Stokes

Paul Hindemith, 2nd Edition (2009)
Stephen Luttmann

Gustav Holst (2011)
Mary Christison Huismann

Charles Ives, 2nd Edition (2010)
Gayle Sherwood Magee

Quincy Jones (2014)
Clarence Bernard Henry

Franz Liszt, 3rd Edition (2009)
Michael Saffle

Alma Mahler and Her Contemporaries (2017)
Susan M. Filler

Bohuslav Martinů (2014)
Robert Simon

Felix Mendelssohn Bartholdy, 2nd Edition (2011)
John Michael Cooper with Angela R. Mace

Olivier Messiaen, 2nd Edition (2017)
Vincent P. Benitez

Nikolay Andreevich Rimsky-Korsakov, 2nd Edition (2015)
Gerald R. Seaman

Gioachino Rossini, 2nd Edition (2010)
Denise P. Gallo

Ralph Vaughan Williams (2016)
Ryan Ross

Giuseppe Verdi, 2nd Edition (2012)
Gregory W. Harwood

Richard Wagner, 2nd Edition (2010)
Michael Saffle

Anton Webern (2017)
Darin Hoskisson

GENRES

Blues, Funk, R&B, Soul, Hip Hop, and Rap (2010)
Eddie S. Meadows

Chamber Music, 3rd Edition (2010)
John H. Baron

Choral Music, 2nd Edition (2011)
Avery T. Sharp and James Michael Floyd

Church and Worship Music in the United States, 2nd Edition (2017)
Avery T. Sharp and James Michael Floyd

Ethnomusicology, 2nd Edition (2013)
Jennifer C. Post

Free Jazz (2018)
Jeffrey Schwartz

The Madrigal (2012)
Susan Lewis Hammond

The Musical, 2nd Edition (2011)
William A. Everett

North American Fiddle Music (2011)
Drew Beisswenger

Piano Pedagogy (2009)
Gilles Comeau

Popular Music Theory and Analysis (2017)
Thomas Robinson

The Recorder, 3rd Edition (2012)
Richard Griscom and David Lasocki

String Quartets, 2nd Edition (2011)
Mara E. Parker

Women in Music, 2nd Edition (2011)
Karin Pendle and Melinda Boyd

Alma Mahler and Her Contemporaries
A Research and Information Guide

Susan M. Filler

ROUTLEDGE MUSIC BIBLIOGRAPHIES

NEW YORK AND LONDON

First published 2018
by Routledge
605 Third Avenue, New York, NY 10017

and by Routledge
2 Park Square, Milton Park, Abingdon, Oxon, OX14 4RN

First issued in paperback 2021

Routledge is an imprint of the Taylor & Francis Group, an informa business

Copyright © 2018 Taylor & Francis

The right of Susan M. Filler to be identified as author of this work has been asserted by her in accordance with sections 77 and 78 of the Copyright, Designs and Patents Act 1988.

All rights reserved. No part of this book may be reprinted or reproduced or utilised in any form or by any electronic, mechanical, or other means, now known or hereafter invented, including photocopying and recording, or in any information storage or retrieval system, without permission in writing from the publishers.

Trademark notice: Product or corporate names may be trademarks or registered trademarks, and are used only for identification and explanation without intent to infringe.

Publisher's Note
The publisher has gone to great lengths to ensure the quality of this reprint but points out that some imperfections in the original copies may be apparent.

Library of Congress Cataloging-in-Publication Data
A catalog record for this book has been requested

ISBN 13: 978-1-03-223665-0 (pbk)
ISBN 13: 978-1-138-93014-8 (hbk)

DOI: 10.4324/9781315680712

Typeset in Minion
by codeMantra

Contents

Acknowledgements	*vii*
Postscript	*ix*
Introduction	1

	Entry No.
I. General	
Reference Books	1–11
Historical Context	12–18
Biographical	19–26
Musico-Analytical	
Scores and Editions	27–29
II. Alma Maria Schindler Mahler-Werfel	
Reference Books	30–33
Historical Context	34–39
Biographical	40–91
Musico-Analytical	
Analytic Essays and Articles	92–104
Scores and Editions	105–116
III. Florence Beatrice Price	
Reference Books	117–125
Biographical	126–141
Musico-Analytical	
Analytic Essays and Articles	142–155
Scores and Editions	156–172
IV. María Teresa Prieto Fernández de la Llana	
Reference Books	173–181
Historical Context	182–191
Biographical	192–202
Musico-Analytical	
Scores and Editions	203–218

v

V. **Yuliya Lazarevna Veysberg**

    Reference Books   219–230
    Historical Context   231–275
    Biographical   276–290
    Musico-Analytical
        Scores and Editions   291–307

Index of Authors, Editors and Translators   *page 77*

Acknowledgements

I would like to acknowledge the assistance of Constance Ditzel, my editor at Routledge, who suggested this book and patiently answered all questions I raised in the research and writing process. Additionally, I want to thank several colleagues who encouraged me with their assurances that this book was worth the research effort: Elizabeth Keathley, Olga Panteleeva, Karin Pendle and James Briscoe.

The assistance of the staff at the Northwestern University Music Library, the Harold Washington Library (Chicago), the Library of Congress and the Boston Public Library has been unstinting and much appreciated.

My friend Larry Prier has given me much moral support and personal interest in this project, especially the parts about Florence Price, in whom he was especially interested from a historical point of view. My family, especially my parents Robert and Miriam Filler, not only encouraged me with many relevant questions and comments, but with their confidence in my ability to bring this work to a successful end.

This book is dedicated to the memory of Theodore C. Karp, who was my dissertation adviser at Northwestern University, my colleague and my friend. I trust that Judith Schwartz-Karp knows how much he meant to my development as a musicologist.

Susan M. Filler
Chicago, Illinois
September 2016

Postscript

My sister Susan Filler passed away on July 7, 2017 at the age of 69. This book is her final published work in a life dedicated to her passion for musicology. While her early research focused almost entirely on Gustav and Alma Mahler, her interests expanded over her career to include a broader exploration of Jewish music from around the world as well as the generally under-attended work of women composers. She was a remarkably dedicated scholar, engaged in her research passion only after-hours while she worked in hospital administration. When Susan finally retired from her day job, she entered a scholarly renaissance. In addition to this volume, her recent work explored music of early twentieth century Jewish nationalist composers in Russia and nearby Asian regions. Susan left this world in the midst of her (second) prime, something we all might hope to do.

Susan entirely finished this book except for a SUBJECT index. It is a complete work.

Daniel M. Filler
Philadelphia, Pennsylvania
August 2017

Introduction

Women Composers of the Twentieth Century
Alma Mahler and Others of Her Time

This book is a new development of a project that began in the 1980s, when the subject of female composers—whose work had been neglected for centuries—was beginning to gain traction among music historians and performers. I had completed a doctoral dissertation about the source materials for the compositions of Gustav Mahler at Northwestern University, and in subsequent years, I learned for the first time that his wife, Alma Schindler-Mahler, was a composer in her own right, some of whose works were traceable in libraries. In my early work about Alma Mahler, I considered the relationship between her work and that of her husband, a methodology that involved historical context as well as musical style. It was not new in those days, since the relationship of the Mahlers was comparable to the situation of other female composers affected by association with male composers related to them by birth or marriage, e.g. Robert and Clara Schumann, Felix and Fanny Mendelssohn and possibly Wolfgang and Nannerl Mozart.

In the course of research for *Gustav and Alma Mahler: A Guide to Research* (New York: Garland Publishing, 1989), an annotated bibliography of source materials applicable to these composers, I included publications relevant to Alma as well as Gustav Mahler. The late Barry Brook, one of my editors, questioned the plausibility of including Alma, suggesting that this would be allowing her to ride on her husband's coattails. In many respects, I agreed with his reasoning; but I pointed out to him that, given the limited number of published references to Alma's work, a separate book about her was not feasible. Thus, the first edition of the book and, indeed, the revised edition (*Gustav and Alma Mahler: A Research and Information Guide*), which was published by Routledge in 2008, included both composers.

Even then I could see that the literature specific to Alma had increased substantially in the nineteen years between the two editions. This growth has continued to the present day. While published books, articles and editions of her music are still not extensive enough to justify a bibliography entirely devoted to her, it is certainly appropriate for her to be compared with other composers of her time, since she shared with them professional and personal conditions that influenced their lives and work. The time has come for the music of Alma Mahler to be considered in a new context. It is for this reason that I chose three other composers who experienced a problem that affected all their lives: they were female, and, in spite of many improvements in the social rights of women (including suffrage, which was introduced half a century after the abolition of slavery), they lived with sexual discrimination. They were Florence Beatrice Price, an African-American, María Teresa Prieto Fernández de la Llana, a Spaniard who emigrated to Mexico and Yuliya Lazarevna Veysberg, a Russian Jew.

But this is not the only commonality between these four composers. They were all affected by the politics of the twentieth century, including other forms of discrimination. Although they came from different countries and cultures, their work was an active demonstration against religious, racial and class discrimination. Their musical education, whether private or in conservatories in such cities as Madrid, Vienna, St. Petersburg and Boston, was excellent, and in many cases, they were successful in spite of being outnumbered by their male teachers, fellow students and colleagues.

The documented vital statistics of these women's lives are often sketchy. Alma Mahler is the only one for whom we have definitive dates of birth (August 31, 1879) and death (December 11, 1964). Florence Price is known to have been born on April 9, but there is disagreement among biographers about the year (1887 or 1888), which has not been resolved by a birth certificate or church register. There is evidence of the date she died in Chicago (June 3, 1953) through governmental documentation (a death certificate) and newspaper accounts, but the actual location of her grave in Lincoln Cemetery is unmarked.

The exact date of birth of María Teresa Prieto is not documented in any known church register of baptism in the city of Oviedo in the Asturias, where she was born; only the year of her birth (1896) is known. However, the date of her death (January 24, 1982) was noted by public information sources in Mexico City.

Vital statistics for Yuliya Lazarevna Veysberg are particularly difficult to ascertain, especially in the case of her birth data, which is probably confused because of the old Russian system of dating on the Orthodox calendar. For a period during her lifetime it co-existed with the Western calendar. According to different accounts, she was born on December 25/January 6 in either 1878 or 1880 (there are also citations of 1879, which suggest a compromise); a survey of reports from different sources suggests 1878 as likely. It is also worth considering the possibility that she wished to appear younger than she really was. The date of her death (March 1 or 4, 1942) is in doubt because she was among many casualties during the Nazi siege of Leningrad during World War II, rendering detailed records almost impossible under the circumstances. However, her death was reported in several periodicals in the Soviet Union and other countries. Before her marriage to Gustav Mahler, Alma Maria Schindler studied piano and composition privately in Vienna. Her teachers included Robert Gound and Josef Labor, who taught harmony and counterpoint, and Alexander von Zemlinsky, who also numbered Arnold Schoenberg among his students. It is worth noting that she never studied at the

Vienna Conservatory, which was responsible for the education of performers, conductors and composers including Gustav Mahler himself. Nor did Alma study academic musicology at the University of Vienna. In this respect, she was short-changed in her education compared to the other composers discussed in this book. This may have been among the reasons that she is still treated as a second-class composer; another is that her reputation is still more of a *femme fatale* than a composer, and she finalized that priority herself by the life she lived, which included two subsequent marriages and more than one sexual affair. Even today, she is well known for collecting famous men like homemakers collect recipes. She married three of them: Gustav Mahler (who died in 1911), Walter Gropius (from whom she was divorced) and Franz Werfel (who died in 1945), and among many other men with whom she engaged was Oskar Kokoschka. From her marriages, she had four children, of which only one—Anna Mahler, who became a famous sculptor—lived to grow up and have children. A major problem for those who would assess her work as a composer was that these men were so well known that they left personal accounts of their own lives, which included her; those became the basis of public fascination with this remarkable woman's sex life, which her work as a composer could not possibly equal. When she and Werfel left Vienna in 1938, she took with her a cache of manuscript scores of Gustav Mahler but left behind her own compositions, which were destroyed by bombs. This is a compelling demonstration of her own priorities. Although she cited many compositions in her diaries, today, her work is represented by a limited number of songs for voice and piano, most of which survived through publication.

Florence Beatrice (Smith) Price has been widely discussed in sources covering the work of African-American composers, but there are curious *lacunae* in the basic facts including publication of her extensive compositional work, which comprised songs, piano and organ pieces; chamber music; and choral and orchestral works. As an outsider to the black community, I suggest that such problems might be addressed by consideration of her work as a woman composer, among others, whose numbers substantially increased among American and British musical professionals before, during and after her lifetime. She was not the first female composer in the United States; her forebears included Margaret Ruthven Lang, Amy Beach and Gertrude "Ma" Rainey, who was a year or two older than Price. Her successors in the next generation included Louise Talma and Miriam Gideon (both born in 1906), Margaret Bonds (a student of Price) and Vivian Fine (both born in 1913).

María Teresa Prieto was an early example of a female composer from the Spanish-speaking world, which was hardly "liberated" for women in the early twentieth century. She studied with Saturnino del Fresno Arroyo in her home city of Oviedo in the Asturias, and with Benito Garcia de la Parra at the Real Conservatorio Superior de Música in Madrid. Her professional priorities might never have been realized if she had remained in Spain, but she emigrated to Mexico in 1937; that was a blessing in disguise, as that country became her permanent home, center of the most significant part of her musical education and ultimately her entire compositional career. In Mexico City, she studied with the native-born Mexican composers Manuel Ponce, Carlos Chavez and Rodolfo Halffter, who—with his brother Ernesto Halffter—had, like Prieto, immigrated to Mexico from Spain. At Mills College in Oakland, California, she studied during 1946–1947 with the great French Jewish composer Darius Milhaud, who had immigrated to the United States to escape the Nazis. Among her fellow students were William Bolcom, Luciano Berio, Steve Reich and Dave Brubeck. Her own compositions, many of which were published in Mexico City during her lifetime, were primarily in vocal, keyboard and especially orchestral forms; others remain in manuscript.

Yuliya Lazarevna Veysberg, the daughter of Lazar Veysberg, was born in Orenburg, a city in the Ural Mountains in the Asian part of the Russian Empire (later the Soviet Union). She graduated from the St. Petersburg Gymnasium in 1895, and, thereafter, attended the historico-philological faculty at the Women's University. Beginning in 1899, she taught private students in music theory on referral from a student of Nikolai Rimsky-Korsakov. She was admitted to the St. Petersburg Conservatory in 1903. Veysberg stands out from the other composers in this book by virtue of her long work as a composer, choral conductor, musicologist, critic and translator. Like several fellow-students in the classes of Glazunov and Rimsky-Korsakov, she was Jewish; but she appears to have been the only woman among them. (The sisters of her classmate Mikhail Gnesin studied at the Conservatory in Moscow then established the Gnesin Institute, which exists to this day.) During the period 1907–1912, while living in Germany, she also studied with Max Reger and Engelbert Humperdinck. Like other professional Jewish musicians in the Russian orbit, she defied the systematic anti-Semitism that affected the Jewish community by the irony of their education with Russian nationalist composers. But in spite of her excellent education, she contended with sexual discrimination even after the Russian Revolution and the establishment of the Soviet Union. For this reason, I chose to include Veysberg (who was about the same age as Alma Mahler) in this book because she was a successful composer who was highly respected by her male colleagues, like Amy Beach in Boston or Germaine Tailleferre among *Les Six* in Paris.

Three of these composers combined their musical professions with marriage and motherhood. The exception was María Teresa Prieto, who appears to have been entirely devoted to her work. Her brother, Carlos Prieto, initiated their plans for emigration to Mexico during the Spanish Civil War, having himself set the example in 1936 (she joined him a year later). The other composers in this book were married more than once. All of them paid a price for the balancing act between their professional and personal lives. This problem still exists today, in spite of significant progress in law, medicine and politics, as well as music. Such women depend on their own determination, especially when they are affected by the attitude of the men in their lives. One might almost envy Prieto, Ethel Smyth, Louise Talma or Nadia Boulanger, who did not experience such constraints in their families.

Florence Price was a professional woman (she studied at the New England Conservatory of Music, earning teaching credentials in piano and organ) who married a professional husband, with whom she had two daughters. Their decision to move from Little Rock, Arkansas to Chicago in 1927 influenced better consequences for her life and work than it did for his; their marriage broke up. Although she subsequently remarried to Pusey Dell Arnett (1875–1957), who was well known as a baseball player in the "Negro Leagues," they separated a few years later. As in the case of Alma Mahler-Werfel, this was a situation in which the woman was compelled to choose between marriage and a career, and Price's marriages—unlike Alma's—did not stand a chance considering that her commitment to music was the means by which she supported her daughters and established her professional position. She certainly did not gain status from her marriages as Alma Mahler did from hers.

It is unlikely that Yuliya Lazarevna Veysberg, when studying with Rimsky-Korsakov, could have foreseen that she would marry the great composer's son, Andrei, a musicologist rather than a composer. When she did, it was after his father's death during her exile in Germany. During that period, in 1907, she had married the Jewish violinist Leonid Davidovich Kreutser, with whom she had a son, Viktor Leonidovich Kreutser, but this marriage apparently lasted only a few years. She returned to Russia in 1912 and married Andrei almost immediately; they too had a son, Vsevolod Andreevich Rimsky-Korsakov, who was born in 1914. There was no rivalry between her and her husbands; neither of them would have been likely to challenge her work as a composer, choral conductor, musicologist and translator. Apart from her compositions, which were especially devoted to vocal works, operas and orchestral works, she contributed reports to two periodicals (*Russkaya Molva* in 1912 and *Muzykal'naia Sovremennik* in 1915–1917) and accomplished a translation of the musical writings of the French *literatus* Romain Rolland.

The political events of the time in which these composers lived may or may not have worked in their favor. From the beginning of the twentieth century, they lived through the establishment of important rights for women, but these were counteracted by war and other civil unrest—political discrimination based on racial, sexual and religious factors. In the course of their lives, each of them was compelled to leave the homes where they had been born and raised and adjust to the problems of exile in an unfamiliar place. Alma Mahler, who might have been able to stay in Vienna where she had lived from her birth in 1879 until the Nazi takeover of Austria in 1938, emigrated to France and ultimately the United States. She was not in any personal danger, but she chose to stay with her third husband, Franz Werfel, who was Jewish. María Teresa Prieto essentially chose to interrupt her musical education and leave her home forever to live in Mexico, which must have been a major change in mid-life, although it was the best move she could have made in terms of its effect on her work as a composer.

When Florence Price, her husband and daughters moved from Little Rock, Arkansas to Chicago, the action might not have been considered exile, since she did not leave her country (although the strong contrast between Little Rock and Chicago was surely a shock). I define it as exile because she incurred a significant risk by abandoning everything that was familiar to her. The change entailed an important adjustment both personally and professionally. In Chicago, she studied composition with Wesley LaViolette, Carl Busch and Leo Sowerby and performed on the piano and organ (in churches and also in silent movie theaters). This arrangement did not succeed in terms of her personal life, including her marriages, but it was a gamble that worked professionally since her music would probably not be known today if she had stayed in her birthplace. Like Prieto, in that respect, she was successful in her chosen compositional career. Neither she nor Prieto ever returned to live in their original home cities. Alma Mahler-Werfel, too, lived in the United States for the rest of her life but was taken back to Grinzing Cemetery in Vienna for burial.

Yuliya Lazarevna Veysberg returned from Germany in 1912, and she lived in St. Petersburg for the rest of her life. The reason that she interrupted her education at the St. Petersburg Conservatory and spent five years in exile was simple: in 1905, during civil unrest against the government of Russia, she and other students including Mikhail Gnesin were involved in a strike and were expelled from the Conservatory. This was a period of uncertainty for the faculty as well as the students; Veysberg's future father-in-law, Rimsky-Korsakov, resigned from the faculty (as did Glazunov and others), but the period that Veysberg spent in Germany was advantageous not only for her studies and her personal life with her first husband, but also for the contacts she made with publishers including Belaiev (Leipzig) and Universal Edition (Vienna), who subsequently published several of her compositions. Her return to St. Petersburg may have been facilitated by assistance from Glazunov; it was permanent, but the end of her story is a sad one: her second husband died there in 1940, and she and her son, Vselvolod Andreevich Rimsky-Korsakov, died in March 1942 among the casualties of the German siege of the city. There is no answer to the question of her reasons for staying, but we can consider two possibilities: either she made her own decision or she was unable to obtain the necessary papers that would have allowed evacuation. She benefitted from the experience of life outside her original milieu and in that respect gained as much as Florence Price and María Teresa Prieto did.

Each of these composers is heavily represented in the annotated bibliography that follows this essay. All sections include books, articles and essays; theses and dissertations; and musical scores. The bibliography itself is divided into five sections, commencing with materials that are applicable to more than one of my subjects and following with sections devoted to each of them.

The listings are in many different languages besides English, which vary according to the subject in question. Not surprisingly, all materials devoted to Florence Price are in English, and those covering María Teresa Prieto include Spanish as well. The section covering Yuliya Lazarevna Veysberg includes Russian, German and English. A particular problem in the section devoted to Alma Mahler-Werfel is the multiplicity of languages including English, French, German, Spanish, Italian, Magyar, Macedonian and Korean among primary publications. This does not include translations of books that were originally published in Western European languages, which include Chinese, Japanese, Hebrew, Czech, Dutch and many others. There are very few such examples in the sections devoted to the other composers, and this contrast sets Alma Mahler-Werfel apart from them.

With two of these composers, the research process resulted in observations of different typologies important to understanding priorities in the literature. In the case of Alma Mahler-Werfel, there are almost too many biographies (very few of which accord serious attention to her work as a composer) and not enough studies of her music, even after years of development since I first published such materials in 1989. When studying the literature related to Yuliya Lazarevna Veysberg, I noted a preponderance of information in reference books and general histories of the period in which she lived, which surpassed the number of actual biographical accounts. Among these references are several books documenting the life and work of Rimsky-Korsakov, most comprising primary sources including correspondence and diaries; as he and Glazunov (for whom there are also some documentary references) were her instructors, and she married Rimsky-Korsakov's son, they are certainly relevant to a study of the times and milieu in which Veysberg lived. This should not be considered a problem since many studies of music in the Russian orbit emphasize the influence of nationalism on composers whose work is often better known than Veysberg's. As many references are in Russian, I have provided English translations of titles whenever these may be helpful.

The listing of musical scores and editions in this bibliography has proved to be extremely important since many of the works of these composers are not easily available outside libraries and archives. In the instances of Mahler-Werfel, Prieto and Veysberg, inclusion of most or all of their works has been attainable, but the situation is different in the case of Price who composed a very large number of works, many of which are still not published as of this writing. The scores of Price that I listed are a representative selection of works published from her lifetime to the present, including many different *genres*.

Although I have focused primarily on publications in hard copy form, in certain instances, I have included articles and essays available only online.

The tracking of each composer's publishers is a double-pronged challenge, which must be divided into those with whom they worked during their lifetimes and new publishers who have attempted to take advantage of changing copyright laws in different countries. In this respect, information about publication of the works of Alma Mahler-Werfel is unusually straightforward: she worked with only two publishers (Universal Edition and Josef Weinberger, both in Vienna) during her lifetime. Recent editions have been published by:

Bryn Mawr, Pennsylvania: Hildegard Publishing Company
Farmington Hills, Michigan: G.K. Hall/Gale Group
Bloomington & Indianapolis: Indiana University Press

María Teresa Prieto worked with only two publishers in her lifetime:

New York: G. Schirmer
México City: Editiones Méxicanas de Música

A relatively recent publication of several orchestral works of Prieto was released by the Gobierno del Principado de Asturias/Consejeria de Cultura, Comunicación Social y Turismo (Oviedo, Asturias, Spain) and demonstrates a problem that has involved musicologists in both Spain and Mexico: both countries claim her life and work as their own, and this rivalry permeates not only editions of her music, but also secondary literature involved with the subject of her life and the political basis of her music.

Yuliya Lazarevna Veysberg worked with publishers in Russia, Germany and Austria during her lifetime, and several scores were jointly issued by Universal Edition (Vienna), Gosudarstvennoe Izdatel'stvo "Iskusstvo" (Leningrad) and Muzsektor Gosizdata Izdatel'stvo (Moscow). Her first works had been published by M. P. Belaiev, which had been founded in Russia but subsequently moved to Leipzig, Germany. Veysberg's subsequent works were primarily published by Muzgiz (Moscow).

During 1942, a British edition of Veysberg's opera *Gusi-Lebedi* was published in London by The Workers' Music Association—a few years after the original edition in the Soviet Union. The composer's death during that year suggests that this British edition may have been prepared during the last months of her life. In the 1990s, two publishers became involved with specific works of Veysberg: Recital Publications (Huntsville, Texas) and Sikorski (Hamburg, Germany), which publishes a large number of scores by Russian composers of the past and present.

Florence Price, among her many accomplishments, was an savvy businesswoman who essentially acted as her own agent when she needed to make contacts that resulted in performing engagements and publishers for her music. While the list of her publishers below reads like the diary of a nomad, her dispositions in terms of location and typology demonstrate that she knew where to place her works.

New York: Handy Bros. [songs]
Edward B. Marks [songs]
G. Schirmer [songs]
Carl Fischer [piano]
Oxford University Press [piano]
Galaxy Music [organ]

Chicago: McKinley [piano, violin]
Gamble Hinged Music [choral]
Clayton F. Summy (later Summy-Birchard) [choral]

Other: Lorenz (Dayton, Ohio) [organ]
Affiliated Musicians (Los Angeles) [piano]
Theodore Presser (Bryn Mawr, Pennsylvania) [piano]

It is worth noting that Florence Price's old friend and colleague, William Grant Still, established a music-publishing house under his own name in Flagstaff, Arizona, which was responsible for a small collection of her works for piano and organ, a copy of which is filed in the Chicago Public Library. It shows that he not only published her music, but also planned to orchestrate, certain of her piano works.

Other publishers who specialize in music of female composers have included individual works of Price in their catalogs in recent years:

Bryn Mawr, Pennsylvania: Hildegard Publishing Company
Farmington Hills, Michigan: Gale Group/G.K. Hall
Fayetteville, Arkansas: ClarNan
Bloomington & Indianapolis: Indiana University Press

Finally, the publication of the two surviving symphonies of Florence Price by A-R Editions (Middleton, Wisconsin) as a volume of the series *Music of the United States* (under the auspices of the American Musicological Society) was a major accomplishment as the first of Price's orchestral works to be published anywhere.

It is important to note that ClarNan, the publisher in Fayetteville, Arkansas, is closely associated with the availability of the Florence Price Archive in the Special Collections section of the University of Arkansas Libraries. This important collection includes the following materials, which were deposited there in 2010:

Box 1: Correspondence, Diary Fragments, Programs, Other Papers & Photographs

[Series 1] 12 folders

Box 2: Musical Scores [Series 2]

- Sub-series 1 Keyboard (Folder 1, Organ) (Folders 2–4, Piano)
- Sub-series 2 Voice (Folders 5–7, voice with piano) (Folders 8–9, choruses)
- Sub-series 3 Strings (Folders 10–12, chamber music, etc.)

Boxes 3–5: Orchestral Scores, parts, & band arrangement

- Box 3 (Folders 1–9, orchestral scores) (Folders 10–14, parts)
- Box 4 (Folders 1–11, parts)
- Box 5 (Folders 1–7, parts) (Folder 8, band conductor score)

The transfer of this archive to the University of Arkansas might be considered an irony of fate since Florence Price herself never lived in Arkansas again after moving to Chicago; but it might be desirable to regard it as a compensation for the difficult conditions under which black people lived in the age of Jim Crow and the ascendency of the Ku Klux Klan.

Since a considerable number of the musical works of these composers are unpublished or out of print due to the lapse of time, I offer below a listing of repositories that are worth consulting. In the case of Florence Price, there is a substantial collection in the Library of Congress, which appears to include materials not available in the collection at the University of Arkansas: nine recordings, eighteen published scores and—most importantly—eleven manuscript scores, including the *Fantasie Négre in e minor* for piano (1929) and ten songs, most for voice and piano. Four of these songs are listed under Price's *pseudonym* "Vee Jay," which she used in the case of "popular" songs. In addition, there are three unfinished sketches for voice.

The most important archive applicable to Alma Mahler is at the University of Pennsylvania; the bulk of this material is biographical rather than musical. The original manuscript of her *Vier Lieder* (1915), which includes the handwritings of both Gustav and Alma Mahler, is in the collection of Henry-Louis de la Grange in Paris.

Many published scores of María Teresa Prieto are filed in the United States, at the Northwestern University Library and the Indiana University Library. The major repository in Mexico City is the Biblioteca Nacional de México, and other materials are in the possession of Carlos Bousoño Prieto. In Spain, researchers should consult the Biblioteca Nacional de España, the Sociedad Estatal de Commemoraciones Culturales (España), the Orquesta de Córdoba, the Archivio de Música de Asturias and the Comunidad Autónoma Consejeria de Cultura, Comunicación Social y Turismo of the Asturias.

We have no information concerning surviving manuscripts of the works of Yuliya Lazarevna Veysberg, but copies of her most important published works are filed in the National Library of Israel, the British Library, and the following libraries in the United States:

Indiana University Library (Bloomington)
Newberry Library (Chicago)
New York Public Library for the Performing Arts
Free Library of Philadelphia (Edwin Fleisher Collection)
Princeton University Library

For researchers who want to search on-line as well as in libraries, there are two helpful web sites relevant to Florence Price, one of which is the catalog of the University of Arkansas:

- http://libinfo.uark.edu/SpecialCollections/findingaids/price.html
- http://chevalierdesaintgeorges.homestead.com/Price.html23

The vast majority of information about Alma Mahler is found in hard-copy print. I regret that I have not been able to locate reliable web sites that offer information that might supplement or complement books and articles.

There are two web sites that include good information about the life and work of María Teresa Prieto:

- www.mujeresenlamusica.blogspot.com
    (Association of Women in Music of Spain]
- www.arkivmusik.com/classical/album.jsp?album_id=871657

Six web sites include important information about Yuliya Lazarevna Veysberg, especially in searches tracking the history of her own family and that of Rimsky-Korsakov:

- www.museumoffamilyhistory.com/yt/lex/V
- www.encyclopedia.com/article-1G2-2587520785/weissberg-veysberg-julia-lazarevna.html
- www.geni.com/people/Yuliya-Julia-Rimskaya-Korsakova/6000000015698290002
- www.geni.com/people/Andrei-Nikolaevich-Rimsky-Korsakov/6000000014254555507
- http://searchworks.stanford.edu [a listing of two of Veysberg's operas]
- http://america.pink/yuliya-veysberg_4886876.html [including two photographs of Veysberg and others in the Rimsky-Korsakov family]

I
General

REFERENCE BOOKS

1. Block, Adrienne Fried & Neuls-Bates, Carol. *Women in American Music: A Bibliography of Music and Literature.* Westport, Connecticut: Greenwood Press, 1979. xxvii, 303 pp. ISBN: 9780313214103, 0313214107.

    Significant resource for individual musical works by American composers, comprising books, articles, dissertations and scores. Also references databases from important archives.

2. Claghorn, Charles. *Women Composers and Songwriters: A Concise Biographical Dictionary.* Lanham, Maryland: Scarecrow Press, 1996. vii, 247 pp. ISBN: 0780810831308, 0810831309.

    Includes an essay on Florence Price (p. 175), but no entries covering the other three composers discussed in this book.

3. Cohen, Aaron. *International Encyclopedia of Women Composers.* New York: W.W. Bowker, 1981. xviii, 597 pp. Revised edition: New York: Books & Music USA, 1987. 2 vols. ISBNs: 0780961748500, 0961748524; 9780961748524, 0961748516; 9780961748517, 0961748508.

    Entries covering Alma Mahler (vol. 1, p. 441), Price (vol. 1, pp. 462–63), María Teresa Prieto (vol. 1, p. 563) and Yuliya Veysberg [under the spelling "Weissberg"] (vol. 2, p. 746), apostrophizing their lives and compositions. Occasional inaccuracies based on information from some secondary sources, but bibliography allows for contextual comparisons.

4. Gray, Anne K. *The World of Women in Classical Music*. La Jolla, California: WordWorld, 2007. xv, 1055 pp. ISBN: 1599753200.

Divided into four sections: Chapters 1–10 (composers), Chapter 11 (conductors), Chapters 12–13 (performers) and Chapters 14–17 (musicologists and others).

5. Hennessee, Don & Hixon, Don L. *Women in Music: An Encyclopedic Bio-Bibliography*. Metuchen, New Jersey: Scarecrow Press, 1975. xiii, 347 pp. Revised edition: Lanham, Maryland: Scarecrow Press, 1993. 2 vols. [xix, 1824 pp.] ISBN: 0780810827691, 0810827697.

First edition in one limited volume; much enlarged second edition in two volumes, including women in many musical professions. Three of the four subjects of this book are apostrophized in vol. 1: Mahler (p. 686), Price (p. 868) and Prieto (p. 869), while Veysberg (spelled "Weissberg") is listed in vol. 2 (p. 1152).

6. Mayer, Clara, hrsg. *KOM: Komponistinnen im Musikverlag: Katalog lieferbarer Musikalien*. Kassel: Furore, 1996. 274 pp. ISBN: 9783927327290, 3927327298.

Editor is a frequent contributor to publications of Furore Verlag (Kassel, Germany), which specializes in music by female composers. This is a bibliography of books, musical scores and other items from that house.

7. Olivier, Antje & Weingartz-Perschel, Karin. *Komponistinnen von A–Z*. Düsseldorf: Tokkata, 1988. 363 pp. ISBN: 9783980160308, 3980160300.

This book is a predecessor of *Komponistinnen aus 800 Jahren* (see next entry). Comparison of the two books suggests priority of Central and Western European and American composers.

8. Olivier, Antje & Braun, Sevgi. *Komponistinnen aus 800 Jahren*. Kamen: Sequentia, 1996. 475 pp. ISBN: 9783931984007, 3931984001.

Each entry in this book comprises a short biography, list of musical works, bibliography and discography, all in German. Mahler is summarized on pp. 264–66 and Price on pp. 325–26. No references to Prieto or Veysberg.

9. Pendle, Karin & Boyd, Melinda. *Women in Music: A Research and Information Guide*. New York: Routledge, 2010. xxi, 846 pp. ISBNs: 9780415994200, 0415994209; 9780203891209, 0203891201.

Relatively recent among detailed listings of female composers available, comparable to those of Cohen, Hennessee and Hixon, and *Norton/Grove Dictionary of Women Composers*. Essential.

10. Reich, Nancy B. "An Annotated Bibliography of Recent Writings on Women in Music." *Women's Studies/Women's Status*. CMS Report Number 5. Boulder, Colorado: College Music Society, 1988, pp. 1–77.

Good database comprising literature on women in many musical professions including composers; an important source during the early period when

General

research about this subject was in its early stages. Published under the auspices of the College Music Society, it could be greatly expanded if an update were contemplated.

11. Stern, Susan. *Women Composers: A Handbook.* Metuchen, New Jersey: Scarecrow Press, 1978. viii, 191 pp. ISBN: 9780810811386, 0810811383.

   Short entries (a few lines) on each subject. Price listed on page 137 and Mahler (under "Schindler-Mahler") on page 148. No entries covering Prieto or Veysberg.

HISTORICAL CONTEXT

12. Bailey, Brooke. *The Remarkable Lives of 100 Women Artists.* Holbrook, Massachusetts: Bob Adams, 1994. 207 pp.

   Unavailable for examination. Cited in the catalog of the Chicago Public Library but not located in the stacks.

13. Ebel, Otto. *Women Composers: A Biographical Handbook of Women's Work in Music.* Brooklyn, New York: F.H. Chandler, 1902. viii, 151 pp.

   This small biographical dictionary was published very early in the period of the composers discussed in this book. It is worth consulting because of its contemporaneous international documentation of the position of women in the profession such that their social progress can be compared to the literature today.

14. Neuls-Bates, Carol, ed. *Women in Music: An Anthology of Source Readings from the Middle Ages to the Present.* New York: Harper & Row, 1982. xvi, 351 pp. Revised edition: Boston, Massachusetts: Northeastern University Press, 1996. xviii, 400 pp. ISBNs: 9780060149925, 0060149922; 9780060909321, 0060909323.

   Based on documents that offer front-line views of the musicians in question, including personal correspondence and journals, biographies, interviews and contemporary accounts from associates. Little editorial commentary.

15. Olivier, Antje & Weingartz-Perschel, Karin. *Frauen als Komponistinnen. Eine Bestandsaufnahme.* Düsseldorf: Frauenmusikvertrieb, 1987. 189 pp.

   Differs from other books from Olivier in being concise about the position of women among composers. This author's first such contribution, greatly expanded in two additional books listed above (especially the third of 1996).

16. Sadie, Julie Anne & Samuel, Rhian, eds. *The Norton/Grove Dictionary of Women Composers.* London: Macmillan, 1994; New York & London: W.W. Norton, 1995. xliii, 548 pp. ISBN: 9780393034875, 0393034879.

   See individual sections by name of composer for articles covering their lives and work. This book includes versions of some materials previously published in *The New Grove Dictionary of Music and Musicians*, but much is completely new. Evenhanded in coverage of composers in many countries, unlike many other such references.

17. Weissweiler, Eva. *Komponistinnen aus 500 Jahren.* Frankfurt am Main: Fischer, 1981. 401 pp. ISBN: 9783596237142, 3596237149. Revised edition: *Komponistinnen vom Mittelalter bis zur Gegenwart: Eine Kultur- und Wirkungsgeschichte in Biographien und Werkbeispielen.* München: Deutsche Taschenbuch Verlag, 1999. 451 pp. ISBN: 9783423307260, 3423307269.

    In German. Individual essays on composers from the Baroque period to the present do not include Mahler, Price, Prieto or Veysberg, but the author's orientation toward international coverage is rare among references from the German-speaking countries. A good introduction that can be used as a basis for additional research.

18. Zaimont, Judith Lang & Famera, Karen. *Contemporary Concert Music by Women: A Directory of the Composers and Their Works.* Westport, Connecticut: Greenwood Press, 1981. xi, 356 pp. ISBN: 9780313229213, 031322921X.

    Classified list of composers, educators and performers of the twentieth century who contributed their own biographies including lists of works. International focus per support from the International League of Women Composers. Complemented by list of publishers with addresses and a discography.

BIOGRAPHICAL

19. Ammer, Christine. *Unsung: A History of Women in American Music.* Westport, Connecticut: Greenwood Press, 1980. x, 317 pp. Revised edition: Portland, Oregon: Amadeus Press, 2001. 382 pp. ISBNs: 9780313220074, 0313220077; 9780313229091, 0313229090.

    A detailed history of female professional women in American music (composers, performers, conductors and educators) covering the subject chronologically from the colonial period to the present.

20. Bowers, Jane & Tick Judith, eds. *Women Making Music: The Western Art Tradition, 1150–1950.* Urbana: University of Illinois Press, 1987, 2003, 2005. 409 pp. ISBN: 9780252014803, 0363025707.

    Collection of essays by many specialists, addressing chronologically the history of women in musical composition in many countries. Detailed documentation of each and every subject, and overall achievement demonstrates social history covering centuries.

21. Chiti, Patricia Adkins. *Donne in Musica.* Roma: Bulzone Editore, 1982. 200 pp. Revised edition: Roma: Armando, 1996. 415 pp.

    In Italian. Short but significant discussions of Mahler (p. 66), Price (p. 79), Prieto (p. 92) and Veysberg (pp. 94–5). This is highly individual in its approach to the subject matter compared to other such books and rather rare in this language.

22. Cook, Susan C. & Tsou, Judy S., eds. *Cecilia Reclaimed: Feminist Perspectives on Gender and Music*. Urbana & Chicago: University of Illinois Press, 1994. xii, 241 pp. ISBNs: 9780252020360, 0252020367; 9780252063411, 0252063414.

Collection of ten essays, historically rather than biographically oriented. See especially "'A Distinguishing Virility': Feminism and Modernism in American Art Music" by Catherine Parsons Smith (pp. 90–106).

23. Glickman, Sylvia & Schleifer, Martha Furman, eds. *From Convent to Concert Hall: A Guide to Women Composers*. Westport, Connecticut: Greenwood Press, 2003. v, 403 pp. ISBN: 9781573564113, 1573564117.

Coverage of the lives and works of Mahler and Price in the chapter "The Twentieth Century" by Adeline Mueller (pp. 217–343) but no references to Prieto and Veysberg. See also supplemental bibliography, discography and work lists. This book was published during the same period that Glickman and Schleifer were coediting the multivolume anthology *Women Composers: Music through the Ages* and may be considered as companion research to the critical edition (see below).

24. Jezic, Diane Peacock. *Women Composers: The Lost Tradition Found*. New York: Feminist Press, 1988. xx, 250 pp. ISBNs: 9780935312942, 0935312943; 9780935312959, 0935312951. 2nd edition 1994. ISBNs: 9781558610743, 155861074X; 9781558610736, 1558610731.

No specific discussion of the composers included in this book, but useful resource lists for additional searching beyond the limits of its scope.

25. McVicker, Mary F. *Women Composers of Classical Music: 369 Biographies through the Mid-20th Century*. Jefferson, North Carolina: McFarland & Company, Inc., 2011. vi, 253 pp. ISBN: 9780786462186, 0786462183.

Includes all four composers in this book: Mahler (p. 169), Veysberg (pp. 205–06), Prieto (pp. 207–08) and Price (pp. 214–15). More nationalist/geographical than stylistic focus. Useful bibliography on pp. 237–39.

26. Pendle, Karin, ed. *Women and Music: A History*. Bloomington & Indianapolis: Indiana University Press, 1991. x, 358 pp. Revised edition 2004. 516 pp. ISBN: 0780253214225, 025321422X.

Collection of essays covering chronological periods and composers within such guidelines, with some discussion of non-composers as well. Marcia J. Citron includes discussion of Mahler (pp. 133–37) in the section "European Composers and Musicians, 1880–1918." The section "North America Since 1920" cowritten by J. Michele Edwards and Leslie Lasseter features brief references to Price (p. 239) and Prieto (p. 249). Lacking in coverage of Veysberg and other female composers in Russia and other Eastern European composers. Both editions of this book related to collections of music from same publisher (see next section).

MUSICO-ANALYTICAL

Scores and Editions

27. Briscoe, James R., ed. *Historical Anthology of Music by Women*. Bloomington: Indiana University Press, 1987. xii, 402 pp. ISBN: 9780253212962, 0253212960. Revised edition: *New Historical Anthology of Music by Women*. Bloomington & Indianapolis: Indiana University Press, 2004. xiii, 518 pp. ISBN: 9780253216830, 0253216834.

    Important collection of musical works from the Byzantine period to the twentieth century; each entry introduced by critical essays. Contributors chose entries ranging from keyboard and vocal music to chamber and orchestral music. Mahler is included in both editions (her song *Der Erkennende*) and Price in the second edition (*Song to the Dark Virgin*). No examples of music by Prieto and Veysberg.

28. Briscoe, James R., ed. *Contemporary Anthology of Music by Women*. Bloomington & Indianapolis: Indiana University Press, 1997. xii, 404 pp. ISBN: 9780253211026, 0253211026.

    All entries in this collection were composed by living composers, which rules out any of the four subjects of this book. However, the anthology is wide ranging in its contents, musical styles and political orientations, and the introductions to the selections were written by the composers themselves.

29. Glickman, Sylvia & Schleifer, Martha Furman, eds. *Women Composers: Music through the Ages*. Farmington Hills, Michigan: G.K. Hall, 1996–2006. 8 vols. ISBN: 9780783881942, 0783881940 [vol. 7].

    Planned as a twelve-volume anthology of music by female composers in chronological order and typology of music. Eight of the projected volumes had been published when coeditor Sylvia Glickman died in 2006. Vol. 7 and 8 are relevant to this study. Mahler is represented in vol. 7 (devoted to vocal works of the nineteenth century) and Price in both vols. 7 and 8 (large and small instrumental ensembles in which her entry represents chamber music). See sections of this book devoted to those two composers for details. There are no examples of the music of either Prieto or Veysberg in this anthology.

II

Alma Maria Schindler Mahler-Werfel

REFERENCE BOOKS

30. Filler, Susan M. *Gustav and Alma Mahler: A Guide to Research.* New York: Garland Publishing, 1989. li, 336 pp. ISBN: 9780824084837, 0824084837. Revised edition: *Gustav and Alma Mahler: A Research and Information Guide.* New York, London: Routledge, 2008. viii, 408 pp. ISBNs: 9780415943888, 0415943884; 9780203932858, 0203932854.

    Multilingual annotated bibliography covering literature devoted to both Gustav Mahler and Alma Mahler-Werfel. Unlike other bibliographies devoted to musicological literature pertaining to this subject matter, this one is evenhanded as far as possible in terms of inclusion and credit to musicologists from many countries. Objections to items in some languages not in common use have been noted.

31. Vondenhoff, Bruno & Eleonore. *Gustav Mahler Dokumentation, Sammlung Eleonore Vondenhoff: Materialien zu Leben und Werk.* Tutzing: Hans Schneider, 1978. xxii, 676 pp.

32. Vondenhoff, Bruno & Eleonore. *Gustav Mahler Dokumentation, Sammlung Eleonore Vondenhoff: Materialien zu Leben und Werk. Ergänzungs-Band.* Tutzing: Hans Schneider, 1983. 327 pp. ISBN: 379520397X.

33. Vondenhoff, Bruno & Eleonore. *Zweiter Ergänzungsband zur Gustav Mahler Dokumentation: Sammlung Eleonore Vondenhoff / Materialien zu Leben und Werk.* Bearb. von Veronika Freytag. Tutzing: Hans Schneider, 1997. xiv, 305 pp. ISBN: 3795209080.

The above three volumes document the holdings of the Vondenhoff collection, which is now in the Österreichische Nationalbibliothek (Vienna). The first two volumes were compiled with the assistance of the Vondenhoffs themselves. The third was a completion volume when the full collection came to the library on the deaths of the Vondenhoffs. The bulk of the literature in these volumes is in German, numbered consecutively in subject sections arranged in alphabetical order. However, literature in other languages (including English, French, Italian, Dutch, Russian, etc.) is noted in separate sections without numeration or indexing. While most of the literature is about Mahler, Alma Mahler-Werfel is represented in separate sections.

HISTORICAL CONTEXT

34. Brusatti, Otto. *Mahler x 100: von Alma bis Zemlinsky.* Wien: Echomedia, 2010. 269 pp. ISBN: 9783902672247, 3902672242.

    Published for the one hundred fiftieth anniversary year of Mahler's birth. Compiled by the longtime music librarian of the Wiener Stadtbibliothek, who has frequently contributed source studies related to Mahler. References to Mahler-Werfel and other associates in this case are rather unusual in this scholar's contributions.

35. Fry, Varian. *Surrender on Demand.* New York: Random House, 1945. 243 pp. Revised edition: *Assignment Rescue.* New York: Four Winds Press, 1968. 187 pp. 3rd edition: Boulder, [Colorado]: Johnson Books, 1997. xiv, 272 pp. ISBN: 9781555662097, 1555662099.

    The story of the author's work to rescue significant European Jews and political dissidents from the Nazis and bring them to the United States. Alma Mahler-Werfel and her third husband, Franz Werfel, were among those who profited from this assistance in 1940. Worth comparing this account with Mahler-Werfel, Alma's own discussion in *Mein Leben* and *And the Bridge Is Love*, as well as Werfel's introduction to *The Song of Bernadette* (see below).

36. Herrberg, Heike & Wagner, Heidi. *Wiener Melange: Frauen zwischen Salon und Kaffeehaus.* Berlin: Edition Ebersbach, 2002, 2nd edition 2014. 239 pp. (2002 edition), 144 pp. (2014 edition). ISBN: 9783869150932, 3869150939.

    See section "Hofrätin und Muse: Berta Zuckerkandl und Alma Mahler-Werfel."

37. Spielmann, Heinz. *Oskar Kokoschka: Die Fächer für Alma Mahler. Mit einer Umschlagzeichung des Künstlers und einem Vorwort von Lise Lotte Müller.* Hamburg: H. Christians, 1969. 33 pp. Revised edition: Dortmund: Harenberg, 1985. 113 pp. ISBN: 3883794627.

    Exquisite illustrated edition documenting a group of fans that Oskar Kokoschka made as a gift to Mahler-Werfel during their affair, with introductory matter offering a context for these art works in the long career of Kokoschka.

38. Vergo, Peter. *Art in Vienna 1898–1918: Klimt, Kokoschka, Schiele and Their Contemporaries.* London: Phaidon, 1975, 1993; Ithaca, New York: Praeger, 1975, 1981. 256 pp. ISBN: 0714816000. 4th edition: London: Phaidon, 2015. 287 pp. ISBN: 9780714868783, 0714868787. German version: *Kunst in Wien 1898–1918: Klimt, Kokoschka, Schiele und ihre Zeitgenossen.* Hamburg: Edel, 2015. 287 pp. ISBN: 9783944297170, 3944297172.

Beautiful illustrated book documenting the artistic scene in Vienna in the period that Mahler-Werfel was a part of it, especially through her close relations with Gustav Klimt and Kokoschka.

39. Zahn, Leopold. *Franz Werfel.* Berlin: Colloquium, 1966. 93 pp.

Intelligent, well-written German biography of Mahler-Werfel's third husband, in which she is given her due as a personal and professional force in his life. Better balanced than her own account of her relationship with Werfel in her autobiography (see below).

BIOGRAPHICAL

40. An Pyong-uk. *Yonggwaang ui twian kil.* Seoul T'ukpyolsi: Samjinsa, 1972. 276 pp. [In Korean.]

An interesting premise. Comprised of three essays devoted to Clementine Churchill (1885–1977), Mahler-Werfel (1879–1964) and Chiang May-Ling Soong (1898–2003). Apart from being contemporaries who lived long lives with famous husbands (Winston Churchill, Mahler, etc. and Chiang Kai-shek), they established reputations of their own. This book, which precedes a comparable book by Walter Sorells (see below), has never been translated into Western languages.

41. Berger, Hilde. *Ob es Hass ist, solche Liebe?: Oskar Kokoschka und Alma Mahler.* Wien: Böhlau, 1999. 203 pp. ISBN: 9783205991038, 3205991036.

Starts in 1910–1911 with the early work of Kokoschka and the last months of Mahler-Werfel's marriage to Mahler before his death. Continues with coverage of her affair with Kokoschka. Well researched and written, and handsomely illustrated with reproductions of Kokoschka's art and photographs documenting their lives.

42. Blaukopf, Herta. "Alma Mahler." *Österreichische Musikzeitschrift.* 46 (1991): 384.

Short article by insider to Internationale Mahler Gesellschaft (Vienna), who contributed more to research about Mahler than Mahler-Werfel. However, this is not the first example of the author's involvement with the "other Mahler"; compare her introduction to the photo-reprint edition of the fourteen songs of Mahler-Werfel published in the composer's lifetime (see below).

43. Boucher, Agnès. *Alma Mahler, Naissance d'une Ogresse. Récit.* Paris: L'Harmattan, 2013. 217 pp. ISBN: 9782343012087, 2343012083.

    Appears to have grown out of author's book of previous year (see next entry), being entirely devoted to this composer (uncharitably described as a sort of monster). No major new information in this biography compared with others.

44. Boucher, Agnès. *Comment Exister aux Côtés d'un Génie: Fanny Mendelssohn, Clara Schumann, Alma Mahler et les Autres.* Paris: L'Harmattan, 2012. 177 pp. ISBN: 9782296961531, 2296961533.

    Includes Mahler-Werfel in a discussion of female composers affected by the men (husbands, brothers, etc.) in their lives, especially Clara Wieck Schumann and Fanny Mendelssohn Hensel. Basis for such comparison is primarily social, nothing to be gained by comparison of actual musical works.

45. Buchmayr, Friedrich. *Der Priester in Almas Salon: Johannes Hollnsteiners Weg von der Elite des Ständestaats zum NS-Bibliothekar.* Weitra [Austria]: Bibliothek der Provinz, 2003. 336 pp. ISBN: 9783852524610, 385252461X.

    Actually a biography of a Catholic priest in Vienna who became an associate of Mahler-Werfel. She discussed Hollnsteiner extensively in her autobiography and noted that he ultimately left the priesthood and became a Nazi collaborator after the *Anschluss*.

46. Citron, Marcia J. "European Composers and Musicians 1880–1918." *Women and Music: A History.* Edited by Karin Pendle. Bloomington & Indianapolis: Indiana University Press, 1991, pp. 123–41. ISBN: 9780253343215, 0253343216. 2nd edition 2001. ISBN: 9780253214225, 025321422X (see pp. 133–37).

    Well-approached account of Mahler-Werfel as composer in her own right, eschewing comparison with her husband; a *modus operandi* applicable to accounts of all composers in this book who were compelled to live with competition in the family.

47. Colerus, Blanca. "Alma Mahler." *Die Schöne Wienerin.* Hrsg. von Gyorgy Sebestyen. München: Kurt Desch, 1971, pp. 168–82. ISBN: 9783420046193, 3420046197.

    Shows Mahler-Werfel as a product of social norms in Vienna and documents her influence on the growing status of women before there was an organized movement for female rights comparable to those in such other countries as Britain and the United States.

48. Dimoski, Sašo. *Alma Maler.* Skopje: Kultura, 2014. 127 pp. ISBN: 9789989327452, 9989327459.

    In Macedonian. Unavailable for examination, as it has not been translated into Western European languages and is virtually unavailable outside the Widener Library at Harvard University.

49. Escal, Françoise & Rousseau-Dujardin, Jacqueline. *Musique et Différence des Sexes*. Paris: L'Harmattan, 1999. 209 pp. ISBN: 9782738483089, 2738483089.

Mahler-Werfel is included among several female composers (the others being Hildegard von Bingen, Clara Schumann, Fanny Mendelssohn Hensel, Augusta Holmés and Ethel Smyth) who lived different lives according to historical period and marital status. Premise seems to be whether these composers benefitted from independence of men in their lives, which is open to controversy. At least this does not appear to be a discussion of musical style that might be considered "feminine."

50. Franklin, Peter. "Mahler (-Werfel) [née Schindler], Alma Maria." *Norton/Grove Dictionary of Women Composers*, pp. 305–06.

There is no previous version of this entry in the 1980 edition of *New Grove Dictionary of Music and Musicians*, which was the basis for this book and other *Grove Dictionaries* that address specialized subject areas. Fine account of Mahler-Werfel's work from a scholar well known in the literature covering Mahler who does not fall into the trap of comparison between their works.

51. Gallwitz, Klaus, hrsg. *Oskar Kokoschka und Alma Mahler: die Puppe. Epilog einer Passion*. Städtische Galerie im Stäel: Ausstellung vom 6. August bis 18. Oktober 1992. Ausstellung und Katalog Klaus Gallwitz und Stephan Mann. Frankfurt am Main: Die Gallerie, 1992. 112 pp.

Catalog of an exhibition of Kokoschka's works in Frankfurt am Main during 1992, which specifically apostrophized his relationship with Mahler-Werfel and its relevance to his work.

52. Garcia Vila, Antonio. *Alma Mahler: El Fin de una Epoca*. Mataró, [Spain]: Ediciones de Intervención Cultural, 2008. 133 pp. ISBN: 9788496831582, 8496831582.

Concise biography of Mahler-Werfel and her effect on the world in which she lived. Available only in Spanish. A copy is filed at the Stanford University Library.

53. Giroud, Françoise. *Alma Mahler, ou l'art d'être aimée*. Paris: Éditions Robert Laffont, 1988. 260 pp. **English version**: *Alma Mahler, or The Art of Being Loved*. Transl. by R.M. Stock. Oxford & New York: Oxford University Press, 1991. 162 pp. **German version**: *Alma Mahler oder die Kunst, geliebt zu werden*. Aus dem Französischen von Ursel Schäfer. Wien, Darmstadt: Paul Zsolnay, 1989. 205 pp. **Danish version**: *Alma Mahler eller Kunsten at blive elsket*. Oversat fra fransk af Gunner Pedersen. Kobenhavn: Holkenfeldt, 1989, 1992. 214 pp. ISBN: 9788777200618, 8777200616.

In addition to the above editions, this book has been published in Serbian (1988), Portuguese (1989), Finnish (1989), Spanish (1990), Swedish (1990), Hebrew (1992), Italian (1995), Polish (1996), Dutch (2001), Magyar (2001), Romanian

(2003), Chinese (2007), Turkish (2008) and Japanese (n.d.). Title of this book (which has been published in eighteen different languages as of this date) makes it clear that it addresses the woman of the world, not the composer.

54. Giustinelli, Luisella Cassetta. *Le Ragioni di Alma: Una Vita Straordinaria tra Arte e Amore.* Soveria Mannelli, [Italy]: Rubbettino, 2015. 238 pp. ISBN: 9788849844047, 8849844042.

 Recent biography of Mahler-Werfel in Italian, focusing on her remarkable life and interests rather than her work as a composer. At present, the only available copy of this book is in the Widener Library at Harvard.

55. Hilmes, Oliver. *Witwe im Wahn: Das Leben der Alma Mahler-Werfel.* München: 2004. 477 pp. ISBN: 9783886807970, 3886807975. **English version**: *Malevolent Muse: The Life of Alma Mahler.* Transl. by Donald Arthur. Boston, Massachusetts: Northeastern University Press, 2015. 331 pp. ISBN: 9781555537890, 1555537898.

 In addition to the above editions, this book was published in both Dutch and Swedish translations in 2007. This book is a refreshingly irreverent assessment of her character, in contrast with many other biographies.

56. Isaacs, Reginald. *Walter Gropius: Der Mensch und sein Werk.* Transl. by Georg G. Meerwein. Berlin: Mann, 1983–84. 2 vols. **English version**: *Gropius: An Illustrated Biography of the Creator of the Bauhaus.* Boston: Little, Brown, 1991. xix, 344 pp. ISBN: 0821217534.

 The best account of the life and work of Walter Gropius, who was Mahler-Werfel's second husband. A good balance and foil to Mahler-Werfel's own account of their marriage in her autobiography, which cannot always be trusted. Originally planned for publication in English (the author was American), but published first in German. American edition is unfortunately an abbreviated version of the two-volume German prepared after Isaacs died.

57. Kandinsky, Nina. *Kandinsky und ich.* Unter Mitarbeit von Werner Krüger. München: Kindler, 1976. 247 pp. ISBN: 9783463006789, 3463006782. 2nd edition München: Droemer Kaur, 1994. 252 pp. ISBN: 9783426023556, 3426023555. **French version**: *Kandinsky et moi.* Transl. by J.M. Gaillard-Paquet. Paris: Flammarion, 1978. 281 pp. 9782080640130, 2080640135. **Spanish version**: *Kandinsky y yo.* Traducción Cristina Buchheister. Barcelona: Parsifal, 1990. 240 pp. ISBN: 9788487265082, 8487265081. **Turkish version**: *Kandinsky ve Ben.* Francizca'dan çev. Gülnar Öney. Istanbul: Iletişim, 2003. 291 pp. ISBN: 9789750501685, 9750501683. **Italian version**: *Kandinskij e io.* Traduzione di María Teresa Carbone. Milano: Abscondita, 2006. 203 pp. ISBNs: 9788884161291, 8884161290; 9788884162793, 8884162793. **Japanese version**: *Kandinsukī to watashi.* Transl. by Yoshio Dohi & Shukuko Tabe. Tokyo: Misuzushobō, n.d. 364, 7 pp.

This is an eyewitness account of the great artist written by his wife. Mahler-Werfel was an insider to their circle, appearing frequently among secondary personalities.

58. Keegan, Susanne. *The Bride of the Wind: The Life and Times of Alma Mahler-Werfel*. London: Secker & Warburg, 1991; New York: Viking, 1992. xvi, 346 pp. ISBN: 9780670805136, 0670805130. *Spanish version: Alma Mahler: La Novia del Viento*. Transl. by Luis Romano Haces. Barcelona: Paidós Ibérica, 1993, 2003. 350 pp. ISBN: 9788475098654, 8475098657. *Russian version: Nevesta Vetra: Zhizn' i Vremia Al'my Maler-Verfel*. Transl. by Il'i Bassa. St. Petersburg: Kompozitor, 2008. 365 pp. ISBN: 9785737903732, 5737903737.

Comparably better than the biography by Karen Monson a decade earlier, but marred by inaccuracies, and totally lacking in attention to Mahler-Werfel's compositions.

59. Kokoschka, Oskar. *Mein Leben*. Vorwort und dokumentarische Mitarbeit von Remigius Netzer. München: Bruckmann, 1972. 339 pp. *English version: My Life*. Transl. by David Britt. New York: Macmillan, 1974. 240 pp. *Italian version: La Mia Vita*. Transl. by Carmine Benincasa & Andrea Shanzer. Venezia: Marsilio, 1982. xxxv, 216 pp.

Personal account from the artist and dramatist who had an affair with Mahler-Werfel between the death of Mahler and her second marriage to Gropius. They continued to communicate for many years, and his autobiography is a valuable counterweight to many statements in her autobiography.

60. Kostick, Gavin & Deane, Raymond. *The Alma Fetish*. [Dublin, Ireland]: The Contemporary Music Centre Ireland, [2012]. 35 pp.

This is the libretto of a two-act opera about Mahler-Werfel's relationship with Kokoschka. Gavin Kostick was the librettist and Raymond Deane the composer.

61. Koves, Peter. "Gustav és Alma Mahler." *Lege Artis Medicinae*. 21, Part 3 (2011): 232–35.

This article appeared in a medical rather than a musical periodical, suggesting that it was concerned with the health of the relationship between the two composers. This sort of assessment has been found in the literature about Mahler (especially in English and German), but Mahler-Werfel's own medical and psychological history is rarely represented, especially in inaccessible languages (in this case Magyar). Available on demand in the British Library, London.

62. Lee, Ellen. "The Amazing Alma Mahler: Musical Talent, Bountiful Charm, and a Zest for Life." *Clavier* 38, no. 4 (April 1999): 20–23.

Written for musical professionals who might conceivably come across Mahler-Werfel's songs in the course of their work. Strikes a balance between Mahler-Werfel's life and an introduction to her work. Frequent inaccuracies and simplistic assessment of the musical works.

63. Mahler-Werfel, Alma. "Dem Genie die Steine aus dem Weg räumen (1902–1905)." *Frau und Musik.* Hrsg. von Eva Rieger. Die Frau in der Gesellschaft: frühe Texte. Hrsg. von Gisela Brinker-Gabler. Frankfurt am Main: Fischer Taschenbuch Verlag, 1980, pp. 117–26. ISBN: 9783596222575, 3596222575.

This book represents female composers in the German-speaking countries through use of primary documents from the Baroque period to the present. The entry above is excerpted from *Gustav Mahler: Erinnerungen und Briefe.* While it appears to repeat previously published accounts, its use in this book situates Mahler-Werfel in a historical context that is not applicable to the full biography.

64. Mahler-Werfel, Alma. *"Ich möchte so lange leben, als ich Ihnen dankbar sein kann": Der Briefwechsel Alma Mahler, Arnold Schöenberg.* Hrsg. von Heide Tenner. St. Pölten, [Austria]: Residenz, 2012. 301 pp. ISBN: 9783701732654, 3701732655.

Two-way correspondence between Mahler-Werfel and Schoenberg, divided into two main parts: *Europa (Die Briefe 1910–1931)* and *Im Exil (Die Briefe 1934–1951).* Primarily in German with some English. Handsomely illustrated with photographs.

65. Mahler-Werfel, Alma. *Tagebuch-Suiten 1898–1902.* Hrsg. von Antony Beaumont und Susanne Rode-Breymann. Frankfurt am Main: S. Fischer, 1997. xvii, 862 pp. ISBN: 9783100461063, 3100461061. **American edition:** *Diaries, 1898–1902.* Selected and transl. by Antony Beaumont. Ithaca, New York: Cornell University Press, 1999. xix, 494 pp. **British edition:** London: Faber & Faber, 2000. 528 pp. ISBN: 9780801436543, 0801436540. **Dutch version:** *Het is een vloek een meisje te zijn; een keuze uit de dagboeken 1898–1902.* Transl. by Peter Claessens. Amsterdam: Arbeiderspers, 2001. 295 pp. ISBN: 9789029530743, 902953074X. **French version:** *Journal Intime: Suites, 1898–1902.* Transl. by Alexis Tautou. Paris: Ed. Payot et Rivages, 2012. 409 pp. ISBN: 9782743624194, 2743624191.

This is only a fraction of the diaries kept by Mahler-Werfel during her long life, but it covers a very significant period in her life (1898–1902) when she was especially active as a student and composer until her marriage to Mahler. The German edition includes a great deal of information that was omitted from subsequent translations, but the English version does have extensive critical notes by Antony Beaumont. Documentation of many musical works here that she omitted from her biography of Mahler and her autobiography, most of which were destroyed.

66. Mahler-Werfel, Alma. *And the Bridge is Love.* In collaboration with E.B. Ashton. New York: Harcourt, Brace & Company, 1958. 312 pp. London: Hutchinson & Company, 1959. 282 pp. *My Life, My Loves.* New York: St. Martin's Press, 1989. ISBN: 9780312025403, 0312025408. **German version:** *Mein Leben.* Vorwort von Willy Haas. Frankfurt am Main: S. Fischer, 1960, 2000. 376 pp. ISBN: 9783103478006, 3103478003. **French version:** *Ma Vie.* Paris: R. Juillard, 1961. 375 pp. **New French version:** *Ma Vie.* Traduit de Gilberte Marchegay. Paris:

Hachette, 1985. 386 pp. ISBN: 9782010112393, 2010112393. *Spanish version*: *Mi Vida*. Traducción de Luis Romano Haces. Barcelona: Tusquets, 1984, 1987. 361 pp. ISBN: 9788472232167, 8472232166. *Italian version*: *Autobiografia*. Roma: Editori Riuniti, 1985. 335 pp. **New Italian version**: *La Mia Vita*. Roma: Castelvecchi, 2012. 354 pp. ISBN: 9788876157400, 8876157409. *Portuguese version*: *Minha Vida*. Sao Paulo, [Brazil]: Martins Fontes, 1988. 391 pp. *Dutch version*: *Mijn Leven*. Vert. door Willem van Toorn. Amsterdam: De Arbeiderspers, 1989. 451 pp. ISBN: 9789029529839, 9029520830. *Danish version*: *Mit Liv*. Kobenhavn: Hans Reitzels Forlag, 1991. 302 pp. ISBN: 9788741232393, 8741232399. *Czech version*: *Můy Život*. Praha: Panorama/Mlada Fronta, 1993. 373 pp. ISBNs: 9788070382615, 8070382619; 9788020404251, 8020404252. *Bulgarian version*: *Mojat Život*. Transl. by Diana Lazarova. Varna: Stalker, 2014. 334 pp.

The famous autobiography that has been published in ten languages (two editions—each in English, Italian and French). The editions published in her lifetime differed from each other in substantive ways, and in organization, and this problem has worsened with the publication of other editions since her death. We should also take into account many discrepancies between her own accounts and those of close associates including Gropius, Kokoschka and Werfel. Very little about her work as a composer in any case.

67. Mahler-Werfel, Alma. *Gustav Mahler: Erinnerungen und Briefe*. Amsterdam: Allert de Lange, 1940. 480 pp. Rev. Ausgabe (hrsg. von Donald Mitchell) Frankfurt am Main & Berlin: Ullstein/Propyläen, 1971. 392 pp. ISBN: 3549174454. **English versions**: *Gustav Mahler: Memories and Letters*. Transl. by Basil Creighton. New York: Viking Press, 1946; Seattle & London: University of Washington Press, 1968. vi, 277 pp. Revised edition (edited by Donald Mitchell) London: John Murray, 1968, 1969; New York: Viking Press, 1969; Seattle & London: University of Washington Press, 1971. 3rd edition (further enlarged with new appendix and chronology by Knud Martner & Donald Mitchell) London: John Murray, 1973; Seattle & London: University of Washington Press, 1975, 1979. Fourth edition (with additional notes and commentaries by Donald Mitchell & Knud Martner) London: Cardinal, 1990. xl, 369 pp. (1968, 1969 & 1971 editions); 393 pp. (1973 edition); xliii, 399 pp. (1975/1979 editions); xliv, 429 pp. (1990 edition). ISBN: 0747403171, 0295953780.

In addition to the above editions, there are translations in the following languages: Swedish (1948 and 1977), Italian (1960, 1976 and 2010), Czech (1962), Russian (1964), Japanese (1971 and 1973), Spanish (1978, 1979 and 1986), French (1980) and Chinese (2012). The author's first published book—a biography of Mahler and a collection of his letters to her before and during their marriage. Originally in German; published in Amsterdam early in World War II; published in English translation after the war. The multiple editions from Britain and the United States have benefitted from the extensive critical commentaries of Donald Mitchell and Knud Martner. Mahler-Werfel addresses the controversy regarding her own musical works more specifically in this book than in her autobiography (see previous entry), which makes it more valuable for scholars who assess the circumstances of her own career, although there is little detail about individual works.

68. Margarit, Isabel. *Alma Mahler: La gran dama de la seduccion.* Mujeres apasionadas, 20. Barcelona: Planeta, 1994. 208 pp. ISBN: 8408011006.

    Assessment of Mahler-Werfel as a woman in society; one in a series of biographies of individual women who defied sexual standards in their times.

69. Monahan, Seth. "'I Have Tried to Capture You...' : Rethinking the 'Alma' Theme From Mahler's Sixth Symphony." *Journal of the American Musicological Society* 64 (2011): 119–178.

    Raises questions concerning the relationship between the Mahlers during the first years of their marriage, through the medium of Mahler's putative depiction of his wife and children, as well as himself, at different points of the *Symphony no. 6*. Author's argument regarding Mahler-Werfel's account of her husband's creative process during composition raises valid issues about her own problem with Mahler's ban on composition at this stressful period.

70. Monson, Karen. *Alma Mahler: Muse to Genius: From Fin-de-Siècle Vienna to Hollywood's Heydey.* Boston: Houghton Mifflin, 1983. xviii, 348 pp. ISBN: 9780395322130, 0395322138. **British version**: *Alma: A Biography of Alma Mahler.* London: Collins, 1984. 300 pp. ISBN: 9780002163156, 0002163152. **German version**: *Alma Mahler-Werfel: Die unbezähmbare Muse.* Aus dem Englischen von Renate Zeschitz. München: Heyne, 1985. 382 pp. ISBN: 9783453551305, 3453551303. **French version**: *Alma Mahler: Muse de tous les Génies: De la Vienne fin de siècle à l'Hollywood des Années Quarante.* Traduit de William Desmond. Paris: Buchet-Chastel, 1985. 279 pp. **Spanish version**: *Alma Mahler: Musa de Genios: De la Viena de fin de siglo a Hollywood.* Transl. by Hernán Sabaté. Barcelona: Edhasa, 1987. 354 pp. ISBN: 9788435012119, 8435012115. **Turkish version**: *Alma Mahler: Dahilerin esin Perisi.* Transl. by Suna Guler. Istanbul: AFA, 1995. 348 pp. ISBN: 9789754142945, 9754142947.

    Questionable account at best, as the author seems to have been inadequately prepared to write a serious biography. In spite of the fact that she accessed information about the subject that was not available to the public, the book is often inaccurate and is not well organized so as to appeal to a general audience. Scant information about Mahler-Werfel's compositional work (a serious omission considering that the author was a professional music critic). Translations compound errors in the original text.

71. Montero, Rosa. *Historias de Mujeres.* 6th edition. Madrid: Punto de Lectura, 2011. 248 pp. ISBN: 9788466368490, 8466368493.

    See essay "Alma Mahler: Con garras de Acero" (pp. 117–32). Book is devoted to women of the nineteenth and twentieth centuries who were independently active professionally but lived in the shadows of their male associates. Among subjects like Agatha Christie, George Sand, Frida Kahlo, Margaret Mead and the Brontë sisters (active in literary, artistic and political work), Mahler-Werfel is the only musical professional in this group. Short list of references for additional reading at end of each chapter.

72. Nemec, Claudia. *Aus dem Kochbuch der Alma Mahler: die besten Rezepte der berühmtesten Gastgeberindes Alten Wien.* Wien: Seifert Verlag, 2015. 176 pp. ISBN: 9783902924445, 3902924446.

Alternative title: *Almas Küche: Originalrezepte aus dem Kochbuch der Alma Mahler-Werfel.* Based on the original book of recipes Mahler-Werfel collected over many years, which is filed in the Österreichische Nationalbibliothek (Vienna). This is a selection of sixty recipes divided into sections according to types, researched and chosen by a culinary historian from Vienna who appreciates the historical and cultural value of such documents, which were a regular feature in households during Mahler-Werfel's time and after. A unique document in the Mahler-Werfel literature.

73. Peham, Helga. Die Salonièren und die Salons in Wien: 200 Jahre Geschichte einer besonderen Institution. Wien: Styria Premium, 2014. 325 pp. ISBN: 9783222134487.

See chapter "Alma Mahler-Werfel und Anna Mahler," which, as a rarity, accords due attention to Mahler-Werfel's daughter the famous sculptress. Study of the social and intellectual importance of the Viennese salon, of which Mahler-Werfel was a leading light. Knowledge of her often-difficult relationship with her only surviving daughter suggests that Anna Mahler was subordinate to her mother even after they both left Austria and lived outside Austrian society.

74. Perle, George. "Mein geliebtes Almschi..." *Österreichische Musikzeitschrift.* 35 (1980): 2–15.

Comprises seventeen letters from Alban and Helene Berg to Mahler-Werfel, dated from 1927 to 1937. Includes personal, political and professional subjects shared by friends of many years' standing.

75. Phillips, Max. *The Artist's Wife: A Novel.* New York: Henry Holt, 2001. 254 pp. ISBN: 9780805066708, 0805066705.

Curious quasi-autobiography by a male author, in the voice of a female protagonist. No new information was introduced, but it might be appropriate to compare this book with Mahler-Werfel's autobiography.

76. Rieschel, Hans-Peter. *Komponisten und ihre Frauen.* Düsseldorf: Droste, 1994. 234 pp. ISBN: 9783770010288, 3770010280.

Covers nine composers from Christoph Willibald Gluck to Mahler and their relationships with their wives. Appears to suggest progression in social and professional positions affecting marriage over a period of two centuries rather than assessment of possible musical connections.

77. Rietenauer, Erich. *Alma, meine Liebe: Persönliche Erinnerungen an eine Legende.* Wien: Amalthea Signum, 2008. 288 pp. ISBN: 9783850026529, 3850026523.

Eyewitness account of Mahler-Werfel and her family by a little-known member of her circle (born 1924, died 2014), an observer of the Viennese social and intellectual scene.

78. Rode-Breymann, Susanne. *Alma Mahler-Werfel: Muse, Gattin, Witwe. Eine Biographie.* München: C.H. Beck, 2014. 335 pp. ISBN: 9783406669620, 340666962X.

Compare with same author's book of 1999 (see no. 99), which is devoted to analysis of the composer's songs, in contrast with this biography.

79. Roster, Danielle. *Die grossen Komponistinnen: Lebensberichte.* Frankfurt am Main: Insel, 1995. 433 pp. ISBN: 9783458338161. **French version**: *Les Femmes et la Création Musicale: Les Compositrices Européenes du Moyen-Âge au Milieu du XX Siècle.* Traduit de l'Allemande (Luxembourg) par Denise Modigliani. Paris: L'Harmattan, 1998. 350 pp.

Chapters covering the lives of fifteen female composers including Hildegard von Bingen, Nadia and Lili Boulanger, Germaine Tailleferre and Mahler-Werfel. Chronological by design, which is not unusual but remarkably international for a study originally published in German and subsequently translated into French.

80. Sauvat, Catherine. *Alma Mahler: Et il me Faudra Toujours Mentir.* Paris: Payot, 2009. 269 pp. ISBN: 9782228903844, 2228903841.

The second half of the title of this biography suggests that it is an expression of Mahler-Werfel's own opinion about the way she lived her life. This sets it apart from the approach to her story taken by many biographers, especially since her death in 1964, as she is more notorious for her actions than her verbal *ripostes*. This should be compared with her own books, where she did express her own views.

81. Seele, Astrid. *Alma Mahler-Werfel.* Rowohlts Monographien, 50626. Reinbek bei Hamburg: Rowohl Taschenbuch, 2001. 148 pp. ISBN: 9783499506284, 3499506289.

Short biography of Mahler-Werfel in German. Achieves balance between her life and her musical compositions.

82. Sorells, Walter. "Alma Mahler-Werfel: Body and Mind." *Three Women: Lives of Sex and Genius.* London: Oswald Wolff; Indianapolis & New York: Bobbs-Merrill, 1975. pp. 3–69. ISBN: 9780672517501, 0672517507. **Dutch version**: *Drie Vrouwen met Passie en Genialiteit.* Transl. by Aleid Swierenga. Katwijk aan Zee [Netherlands]: Servire, 1982. 240 pp. ISBN: 9789063250782, 9063250789.

Contextualizes Mahler-Werfel's life and work through comparison with those of Lou Andreas-Salomé and Gertrude Stein, three women who independently charted the course of their lives while influencing important men. Possible influence on subsequent studies of Agnès Boucher, Rosa Montero, William Walton and Iannis Xenakis.

83. Steiger, Martina. *"Immer wieder werden mich thätige Geister verlocken": Alma Mahler-Werfels Briefe an Alban Berg und seine Frau.* Wien: Seifert, 2008. 672 pp. ISBN: 9783902406552, 3902406550.

    Compare with article by George Perle (see no. 74), which introduced an important source of information about Mahler-Werfel and the Bergs, who were close to her for many years. This collection, which is much more extensive than the seventeen letters comprised in the article, comprises the other side of the coin, focusing on Mahler-Werfel's own correspondence with them.

84. Torberg, Friedrich. *Liebste Freundin und Alma: Briefwechsel mit Alma Mahler-Werfel.* Nebst einigen Briefen an Franz Werfel, ergänzt durch zwei Aufsätze Friedrich Torbergs im Anhang und ein Vorwort von David Axmann. Hrsg. von David Axmann und Marietta Torberg. München: Langen Müller, 1987. 288 pp. ISBN: 9783784421575, 3784421571.

    Critical edition of correspondence between Mahler-Werfel and the great literatus, supplemented by his correspondence with Werfel. Part of collected edition of Friedrich Torberg's writings.

85. Walton, Chris[topher]. *Lies and Epiphanies: Composers and Their Inspiration from Wagner to Berg.* New York: Boydell & Brewer, 2014. 318 pp. ISBN: 9781580468442, 1580468446.

    In five sections: "Richard Wagner's Dynastic Dreams," "Gustav Mahler's *Resurrection* and the Apostolic Succession," "Of Forked Tongues and Angels: Alban Berg's Violin Concerto," "Wilhelm Furtwängler and the Return of the Muse" and "Here Comes the Sunset: the Late and Last Works of Richard Strauss." Irreverent and thought-provoking assessment of the creative process and how the "muse" affects it. Chapter about Mahler covers pages 31–54.

86. Weidinger, Alfred. *Kokoschka und Alma Mahler: Dokumente einer leidenschaftlichen Begegnung.* München: Prestel, 1996. 122 pp. ISBN: 3791317113. **English version**: *Kokoschka and Alma Mahler.* Transl. by Fiona Elliott. Edited by Jacqueline Guigui-Stollberg. New York: Prestel, 1996. 122 pp. ISBN: 3791317229.

    Short but critical assessment of sources documenting Kokoschka's affair with Mahler-Werfel. Best used as context for autobiographical writings by Mahler-Werfel and Kokoschka themselves, as this book could offer ideas the principals did not.

87. Weissensteiner, Friedrich. *Die Frauen der Genies.* Wien: Deuticke, 2001. 271 pp. ISBN: 9783216306104, 3216306100. **Czech version**: *Zeny Genii.* Transl. by Eduard Světlik. Praha: Nakl. Faun, 2004. 187 pp. ISBN: 9788086275215, 8086275213. **Russian version**: *Zeny Geniev.* Transl. by Ju. Guseva. Moskva:

Tekst, 2008. 205 pp. ISBN: 9785751606312, 5751606310. **Lithuanian version**: *Genijų Moterys*. Transl. by Alfonsas Tekorius. Vilnius: Alma Littera, 2009. 239 pp. ISBN: 9789955380665, 9955380667. **Bulgarian version**: *Ženite na Geniite*. Transl. by Evelina Banev. Sofija: Izdat. Riva, 2012. 160 pp. ISBN: 9789543204052, 9543204055.

This book comprises six chapters, devoted to three wives of composers (Constanze Mozart, Cosima Wagner and Mahler-Werfel), two wives of literati (Christiane Goethe-Vulpius and Katia Mann) and one wife of a scientist (Mileva Einstein). See "Sklavin, Muse und Matrone: Alma Mahler-Werfel," which is in the center of the chronological progression, possibly by design, since these women lived in different historical periods and established their lifestyles in different ways.

88. Werfel, Franz. "Manon." *Erzählungen aus zwei Welten*. Hrsg. von Adolf D. Klarmann. Frankfurt am Main: S. Fischer, 1954. 3. Band, pp. 392–99, 465.

An affectionate portrait of Mahler-Werfel's daughter from her marriage to Gropius, who died in 1935. Werfel had married Mahler-Werfel in 1929, and this memorial to his stepdaughter is worth comparison with Mahler-Werfel's own account in her autobiography. Alban Berg dedicated his last completed work, the *Violin Concerto*, to Manon's memory; this essay is little known by comparison.

89. Werfel, Franz. "A Personal Preface." *The Song of Bernadette*. Transl. by Ludwig Lewisohn. Garden City, New York: SunDial Press, 1942, pp. 5–7. **British version**: London: Pan Books, Lille printed, 1950. **Chinese version**: *Sheng nii zhi ge*. Transl. by Zhang Xiuya. Xiangang: Xinsheng Chubanshe, 1952. 4, 4, 419 pp. **Second Chinese version**: Taibei Shi: Da dichu ban she, min guo 76 (1987). 2, 2, 4, 4, 459 pp.

The introduction to this famous novel, which Werfel wrote after he and Mahler-Werfel escaped the Nazis who occupied France in 1940, gives his own personal view of the circumstances in which they visited the site of Bernadette's purported visions during their odyssey. Autobiographical in a different sense from Mahler-Werfel's own account.

90. Wessling, Berndt W. *Alma: Gefährtin von Gustav Mahler, Oskar Kokoschka, Walter Gropius, Franz Werfel*. Düsseldorf: Claassen, 1983. 303 pp. ISBN: 3546495934. **Spanish version**: *Alma: Compañera de Gustav Mahler, Oskar Kokoschka, Walter Gropius, y Franz Werfel*. Transl. by Karen Stadtlander. Barcelona: Ed. de Nuevo Arte Thor, 1984. 294 pp. ISBN: 8473270940.

Basis of this study generally comprises quotations without critical documentation. There is no information on Mahler-Werfel's musical works. Arrangement of text in sections is a problem.

91. Xenakis, Françoise. "Alma Schindler, 1880–1964." *Zut, On a Encore Oublié Madame Freud...* Paris: Jean-Claude Lattès, 1985, pp. 191–276. **Greek version**: *Na*

Parei Hē Orgē Pali Xechasame tēn Kyria Phrount. Transl. by Manōlē Petala. Athena: Chatzēnikole, 1986. 244 pp. ***Danish version***: *Pokkers Osse: Nu Har Vi Igen Glemt Fru Freud.* Transl. by Eva Høybye. Kobenhavn: Lina, 1987. 191 pp. ISBN: 9788772500249, 8772500247. ***Spanish version***: *Me Casé con un Genio.* Transl. by César Suarez. Madrid: Espasa-Calpe, 1987. 222 pp. ISBN: 9788423924240, 8423924246. ***Portuguese version***: *Ih. Esqueceram Madame Freud.* Transl. by Setsuko Ono. Rio de Janeiro: Rocco, 1987. 227 pp. ***German version***: *Frau Freud ist wieder Mal vergessen worden: Fünf (fast) erfundene Biographien.* München: Knaur, 1988. 317 pp. ISBN: 9783426015698, 8423924246. ***Swedish version***: *Geniets Bättre Hälft: Fem Kvinnoporträtt.* Transl. by Marie Werup. Stockholm: Natur och Kultur/Lund: Btj, 1989. 246 pp. ISBN: 9127017494. ***Hebrew version***: *Le-khol ha-Ruhot Shuv Shakkahnu et ha-Geveret Froid.* Transl. by Hagit Bat-Ada. Tel Aviv: Zemorah-Bitan, 1994. 234 pp.

This book is an entry in a series of popular biographies of women who married important men. The chapter covering Mahler-Werfel is primarily devoted to commentaries on her correspondence and diaries covering the period 1901–1911. As this covers her marriage to Mahler rather than her long life involving other men, it is circumscribed.

MUSICO-ANALYTICAL

Analytic Essays and Articles

92. Filler, Susan M. "A Composer's Wife as Composer: The Songs of Alma Mahler." *Journal of Musicological Research* 4 (1983): 427–42.

    Comparable to article of Robert Schollum (see below) in stylistic analysis of all songs by Mahler-Werfel known at the time of publication. This essay is partially based on program notes the author provided for a recital of Mahler-Werfel songs by Lorna Myers at the 1980 Ravinia Festival. Additional information about other compositions was published in subsequent CDs and critical editions.

93. Follet, Diane. "Redeeming Alma: The Songs of Alma Mahler." *College Music Symposium* 44 (2004): 28–42.

    Apostrophizes *Die stille Stadt* (the first song of *Fünf Lieder*) as an example of the connection between the woman and the composer. Few assessments of Mahler-Werfel's compositions make any attempt to connect them with the course of her life (the article by Jörg Rothkamm below is a rare exception). This article is rather simplistic but thought provoking.

94. Geralds, Marion. "'Bei dir ist es traut': die Lieder von Alma Schindler-Mahler und ihre existentielle Bedeutung für Gustav Mahler." *Gustav Mahler und die musikalische Moderne.* Hrsg. von Arnold Jacobshagen. Stuttgart: Franz Steiner Verlag, 2011, pp. 131–43.

Comparatively recent assessment of Mahler-Werfel as composer in a collection of essays primarily focused on the composer's husband. Interesting premise that Mahler himself was affected by his wife's "modernist" orientation, especially in view of her association with the composers of the Second Viennese School.

95. Grönke, Kadja. "Contrasting Concepts of Love in Two Songs by Alma Schindler (-Mahler) and Gustav Mahler." *Women and the Nineteenth Century Lied.* Edited by Aisling Kenny & Susan Wollenberg. Farnham, Surrey [England] & Burlington, Vermont [USA]: Ashgate, 2015, pp. 217–29.

Interdisciplinary studies of female composers of solo songs beginning in the nineteenth century, including Fanny Mendelssohn Hensel, Clara Schumann and Mahler-Werfel. Author's decision to compare songs of Mahler-Werfel and her husband is risky, since most specialists in her music (including the present author) view her work on her own terms and consider such comparisons to be a disservice to both composers—a view shared by scholars addressing the work of Schumann and Hensel.

96. Kravitt, Edward F. "The Lieder of Alma Maria Schindler-Mahler." *Music Review* 49 (1988): 190–204.

Considers the effect of Mahler-Werfel's musical education on the style of her songs and her choice of texts for her songs, which is considerably more modernist than the choices made by Mahler. Assessment of research on these songs is comparable to the work of Susan M. Filler and Schollum in thoroughness.

97. Mahony, Patrick. "Alma Mahler-Werfel." *Composer*, no. 45 (Autumn 1972): 13–17.

Brief account of Mahler-Werfel by a British associate who stood outside the circle of friends usually highlighted in other literature. Some factual inaccuracies.

98. Martner, Knud. "Verwelkte Blütenträume: die Werke Alma Maria Schindlers. Ein Werkverzeichnis nebst Beiträgen zur Biographie." Unpublished manuscript, 1999. 100 pp.

Unpublished as of this date. One of three references attempting a comprehensive account of all musical works of Mahler-Werfel; the others are the diaries of 1898–2002 (edited by Beaumont and Susanne Rode-Breymann) and the listing compiled by Nadine Sine in *Women Composers: Music Through the Ages* (vol. 7), which she coedited with Filler as introduction to the critical edition of *Vier Lieder* (see next section).

99. Rode-Breymann, Susanne. *Die Komponistin Alma Mahler-Werfel.* [Hannover]: Nieder-sächsische Staatstheater Hannover, 1999. 158 pp. ISBN: 9783931266066, 3931266060.

Comprises six chapters, more biographical than analytical, but good as cultural/historical study of the musical works. References to other scholarly research almost entirely in German literature, lacking significant information in Britain and the United States.

100. Rothkamm, Jörg. "Wer komponierte die unter Alma Mahlers veröffentlichten Lieder? Unbekannte Briefe der Komponistin zur Revision ihrer Werke im Jahre 1910." *Die Musikforschung*. 53 (2000): 432–445.

Author's argument favors Mahler's influence on Mahler-Werfel's compositions. This premise is risky at best, considering the long hiatus between her early studies with Alexander Zemlinsky before her marriage and the resumption of her work a decade later; it also does not allow for possible composition after Mahler's death. While Colin and David Matthews orchestrated several songs from the first two books of 1910 and 1915 (possibly with such a connection between the two composers in mind), this is difficult to prove.

101. Schollum, Robert. "Die Lieder von Alma Maria Schindler-Mahler." *Österreichische Musikzeitschrift*. 34 (November 1979): 544–51.

Comprehensive stylistic assessment of all known published songs of the composer, in German. Musical examples illustrating premises from the first two books (published in 1910 and 1915), but none from the third book published in 1924, a curious omission. Worth comparison with English article by Filler (published independently with no communication between these two authors); both cited by other scholars including Juliane Urban and Rode-Breymann in German, and Marcia Citrin and Peter Franklin in English.

102. Smith, Warren Storey. "The Songs of Alma Mahler." *Chord and Discord* 2 (1950): 74–78.

Early study of Mahler-Werfel as composer, which includes the first two books of songs but not the third. Unfortunately lacking in musical examples, possibly due to the fact that it was published in Mahler-Werfel's lifetime when the materials were presumably still in copyright.

103. Tomlinson-Brown, Rebecca Hanna. "Unmaking Desire: The Lieder of Alma Schindler-Mahler in Performance." [D.M.A. thesis], University of California at Los Angeles, 2003. viii, 62 pp.

Argues that *modus operandi* in the performance of these songs should be linked to Mahler-Werfel's sex life. This is comparable to Diane Follet's opinion about the connection between life and compositions (see above) but is based on multiple examples instead of a single song.

104. Urban, Juliane. "Die Lieder von Alma Mahler-Werfel geb. Schindler (1879–1964)." M.M. thesis, Freie Universität Berlin, 1994. 97 pp.

Remarkably detailed stylistic analysis of all known songs of Mahler-Werfel, without speculation about the composer's life as an influence on the creative process.

Scores and Editions

105. Filler, Susan M. "Alma Mahler: *Der Erkennende*." *Historical Anthology of Music by Women*. Edited by James R. Briscoe. Bloomington: Indiana University Press, 1987, pp. 245–47. ISBN: 9780253216830, 0253212960. Revised edition: *New Historical Anthology of Music by Women*. Edited by James R. Briscoe. Bloomington & Indianapolis: Indiana University Press, 2004, pp. 289–91. ISBN: 9780253216830, 0253216834.

    Republication of the third song in *Fünf Gesänge* (first published in 1924) as an entry in a chronological collection of compositions in many different genres by female composers. Selected not only as an example of the composer's style, but also for biographical reasons, since the text was an early work of Mahler-Werfel's future husband Werfel. Preceded by an introductory essay with relevant information about other musicological literature, which was augmented in the second edition of this collection.

106. Kimball, Carol, ed. *Women Composers: A Heritage of Song*. Milwaukee: Hal Leonard, 2004. 212 pp. ISBN: 9780634078705, 0634078704.

    Collection of songs by female composers, including four of Mahler-Werfel's *Fünf Lieder* (1910): "Bei dir ist es traut," "Ich wandle unter Blumen," "Laue Sommernacht" and "Die stille Stadt." No explanation for omission of "In meines Vaters Garten," the second of the original five songs.

107. Mahler-Werfel, Alma. *Fünf Lieder*. Wien: Universal Edition, 1910. 17 pp.
    - *Die stille Stadt*
    - *In meines Vaters Garten*
    - *Laue Sommernacht*
    - *Bei dir ist es traut*
    - *Ich wandle unter Blumen*

108. Mahler-Werfel, Alma. *Vier Lieder*. Wien: Universal Edition, 1915. 12 pp.
    - *Licht in der Nacht*
    - *Waldseligkeit*
    - *Ansturm*
    - *Erntelied*

109. Mahler-Werfel, Alma. *Fünf Gesänge*. Wien: Josef Weinberger, 1924. 20 pp.
    - *Hymne*
    - *Ekstase*
    - *Der Erkennende*
    - *Lobgesang*
    - *Hymne an die Nacht*

Photo reprint of all songs in the above three books (with introduction in German and English by Herta Blaukopf) Wien: Universal Edition, 1984. v, 49 pp.

The above entries comprise the three known books of songs by Mahler-Werfel published in her lifetime and a photo reproduction of all songs in a single volume, published about the same time as the studies by Schollum and Filler. Herta Blaukopf, an active researcher at the Internationale Mahler Gesellschaft (Vienna) did not attempt to add new information in her introductory summary.

110. Mahler-Werfel, Alma. *Two Lieder [aus dem Zyklus "Mütter" von Rainer Maria Rilke]*. Edited by Susan M. Filler. Bryn Mawr, Pennsylvania: Hildegard Publishing Company, 2000. [4], 13 pp.

Two early songs dating from the period when the composer was studying composition privately with Zemlinsky in Vienna, before her marriage to Mahler. Text of first song is cited in the critical edition of the works of Rainer Maria Rilke, but text of the second song is not, leaving a *lacuna* for subsequent study. Publisher long known for specializing in the music of female composers.

111. Mahler-Werfel, Alma. *Four Early Songs*. Orchestrated by Mufrida Bell. N.P.: n.p., 1991. 2 vols.

Copy of manuscript at the Stanford University Libraries. Unavailable to present author for study. Title raises a question about which songs were chosen for orchestration by Bell.

112. Mahler-Werfel, Alma. *Sieben Lieder: für mittlere Stimme und Orchester*. Orchestrierte von Colin Matthews & David Matthews. Wien: Universal Edition, 1996. 78 pp.

- *Die stille Stadt*
- *Laue Sommernacht*
- *In meines Vaters Garten*
- *Bei dir ist es traut*
- *Licht in der Nacht*
- *Waldseligkeit*
- *Erntelied*

The first four songs are from *Fünf Lieder* (1910) and the last three from *Vier Lieder* (1915). Both of the Matthews brothers are composers in their own right, having first come to public attention during collaboration with Deryck Cooke on his performing version of Mahler's *Tenth Symphony*. It is possible that these songs were chosen because the time that Mahler-Werfel composed them was proximate to the period when Mahler worked on the symphony; comparison of the Matthews' orchestration of these songs might demonstrate cross-references with Mahler's own orchestration in the symphony.

113. Mahler-Werfel, Alma. *Vier Lieder*. Critical edition coedited by Nadine Sine and Susan M. Filler. *Women Composers: Music Through the Ages, vol. 7 [Composers Born 1800–1899: Vocal Music]*. Edited by Sylvia Glickman & Martha Furman Schleifer. New York: Gale Group, 2004, pp. 640–71. ISBN: 9780783881942, 0783881940.

A critical edition of the second book of Mahler-Werfel's songs published in 1915. This was occasioned by the location of a manuscript score of the songs in the collection of Henry-Louis de la Grange (Paris), combining the hands of both Mahler and Mahler-Werfel, which—on comparison with the published edition—demonstrated significant differences, necessitating an exhaustive study coedited by Sine and Filler. The only edition of Mahler-Werfel's music that sums up what we know of works that cannot otherwise be traced today.

114. Mahler, Gustav. *Adagietto [from Symphony no. 5]. Facsimile/Documentation/Recording.* Edited by Gilbert Kaplan. New York: Kaplan Foundation, 1992. 109, [17 & 17] pp. ISBN: 9780571513222, 0571513220.

Includes comparative scores of the *Adagietto* in the hands of Mahler and Mahler-Werfel. Demonstrates Mahler-Werfel's work as copyist for many of Mahler's manuscripts after their marriage in 1902, of which this symphony was the first such example.

115. Mahler, Gustav. *Ich bin der Welt abhanden gekommen. Facsimile edition of the Autograph Manuscripts.* Edited by Gilbert Kaplan. New York: Kaplan Foundation, 2015. 91, [2] pp. ISBN: 9780974961392, 0974961396.

Pages 83–90 comprise a *Stichvorlag* of the song by Mahler-Werfel (incomplete) for comparison with Mahler-Werfel's own sketches, piano and orchestral scores. This entry and the preceding one are the only examples of publication that shows Mahler-Werfel's musical handwriting, which demonstrates the difference from that of her husband.

116. Rieger, Eva & Walter, Käte, hrsg. *Frauen komponieren: 25 Lieder für Singstimme und Klavier.* Mainz & New York: B. Schotts Söhne, 1992. 69 pp.

Collection of songs by ten female composers from the German-speaking countries, covering the classical period to the twentieth century. Mahler-Werfel's songs *Die stille Stadt* and *Ich wandle unter Blumen* (from *Fünf Lieder* of 1910) are the last songs in this publication.

III

Florence Beatrice Price

REFERENCE BOOKS

117. Brown, Rae Linda. *Music, Printed and Manuscript, in the James Weldon Johnson Memorial Collection of Negro Arts and Letters: An Annotated Catalog.* New York: Garland Publishing, 1982. xxiii, 322 pp. ISBN: 0824093198.

    Catalog entries of original manuscript sources, published anthologies and individual works by black composers. Two entries reference works of Florence Price: no. 105 (p. 33) in "Manu-scripts" section and no. 883 (pp. 235–36) in "Individual Works." This is an early harbinger of the many contributions Rae Linda Brown has made to the study of the life and works of Price.

118. de Lerma, Dominique-René, ed. *Bibliography of Black Music.* Westport, Connecticut: Greenwood Press, 1981. 4 vols. ISBNs: 9780313213403, 0313213402; 9780313231445, 0313231443; 9780313242298, 0313242291; 9780313235108, 0313235104.

119. Floyd, Samuel A., Jr., ed. *International Dictionary of Black Composers.* Chicago & London: Fitzroy Dearborn, 1999. 2 vols. ISBN: 9781884964275, 1884964273.

    Article on Price by Brown.

120. Floyd, Samuel A., Jr. & Reisser, Marsha J. *Black Music Biography: An Annotated Bibliography.* White Plains, New York: Kraus International Publications, 1987. xxvi, 302 pp. ISBN: 9780527301583, 0527301582.

121. Floyd, Samuel A., Jr. & Reisser, Marsha J. *Black Music in the United States: An Annotated Bibliography of Selected References and Research Materials.*

Millwood, New York: Kraus International Publications, 1983. xv, 234 pp. ISBN: 9780527301644, 0527301647.

122. Skowronski, Jo Ann. *Black Music in America: A Bibliography.* Metuchen, New Jersey: Scarecrow Press, 1981. ix, 723 pp. ISBN: 0810814439.

All of the preceding five entries by Dominique-René de Lerma; Samuel A. Floyd and Marsha J Reisser; and Jo Ann Skowronski are exhaustive contributions to documentation of sources for the study of black composers and other musicians in the United States. While there are many overlaps, all of them should be used by researchers.

123. Skowronski, Jo Ann. *Women in American Music: A Bibliography.* Metuchen, New Jersey: Scarecrow Press, 1978. vii, 183 pp. ISBN: 0810811057.

An early contribution to the literature about female musicians in the United States. Same author noted in preceding entry for documentation to bibliographic research into black music, but this stands apart in spite of some cross-references.

124. Smith, Jessie Carney, ed. *Notable Black American Women.* Detroit: Gale Research, 1992–2003. 3 vols. ISBNs: 9780810347496, 0810347490; 9780810391772, 0810391775; 9780787664947, 0787664944.

Collection of biographical essays comprising subjects in many different professions including music. Basic information in each entry with references to other source materials. The essay about Price is in vol. 1.

125. Southern, Eileen. *Biographical Dictionary of Afro-American and African Musicians.* Westport, Connecticut: Greenwood Press, 1982. xvii, 478 pp. ISBN: 0313213399.

Exhaustive study covering black composers, conductors, singers, instrumentalists and educators. Ordered alphabetically by personal names; each entry includes a bibliography and, where applicable, discography. Developed independently of Eileen Southern's previous *The Music of Black America* (see below).

BIOGRAPHICAL

126. Abdul-Rahim, Raoul. "Black Women in Music." *Blacks in Classical Music.* New York: Dodd, Mead, 1977, pp. 51–57.

This book is divided into segments covering composers, singers, operas and opera companies, keyboard artists, instrumentalists, conductors (orchestral and choral), divertissements and attitudes. See chapter "Black Women in Music" (pp. 51–57), in the course of which Price is discussed in the section "Composers." Her student, colleague and friend Margaret Bonds is included immediately following.

127. Absher, Amy. *The Black Musician and the White City: Race and Music in Chicago, 1900–1967.* Ann Arbor, Michigan: University of Michigan Press, 2014. xi, 202 pp. ISBNs: 9780472119172, 0472119176; 9780472029983, 0472029983.

"An exploration of the history of African American musicians in Chicago during the mid-20th century." Chapter 1, "Musicians and the Segregated City" (pp. 16–47) and Chapter 2, "From South to South Side" (pp. 48–81) include the period when Price lived in Chicago (1927–1953) and was especially active as a composer, beyond her previous work as teacher, pianist and organist, which continued after the migration. Published when the black community in Chicago was preoccupied with the influence of its history on current problems.

128. Bonds, Margaret. "A Reminiscence." *International Library of Negro Life and History: The Negro in Music and Art.* Compiled & edited by Lindsay Patterson. New York: Publishers Company, 1969, pp. 190–193. xvi, 304 pp.

Eyewitness account from the composer/pianist who studied with Price while they lived in the same house after the breakup of Price's marriage. Price is situated in historical context with comparative references to Harry Burleigh, Marian Anderson, Nadia Boulanger and others.

129. Brown, Rae Linda. *The Life and Work of Florence B. Price.* Urbana, Illinois: University of Illinois Press, n.d.

This book has been cited as "forthcoming" for many years. It is possible that materials from the author's research were channeled into her many other publications about Price.

130. Brown, Rae Linda. "William Grant Still, Florence Price, and William Dawson: Echoes of the Harlem Renaissance." *Black Music in the Harlem Renaissance: A Collection of Essays.* Edited by Samuel A. Floyd, Jr. Westport, Connecticut: Greenwood Press, 1990, pp. 1–86. ISBN: 9780313265464, 0313265461.

The coverage of Price is primarily found on pages 78–86. One of the few studies of Price to consider her professional position in connection with her sex as well as her race. Price and William Grant Still were friends and colleagues for many years, and he was involved in the publication of some of her musical works during her lifetime. Her relationship with William Dawson is not well known.

131. Brown, Rae Linda, Nachman, Myrna S. & Jackson, Barbara Garvey. "Price [née Smith], Florence Bea(trice)." *Norton/Grove Dictionary of Women Composers,* pp. 374–75.

No previous version of this article in the 1980 edition of *New Grove Dictionary of Music and Musicians,* but doubtless related to other research published by this author.

132. *Composer Florence Price: To be Young, Gifted and Black in a Jim Crow Era.* http://womensvoicesforchange.org/tag/florence-price [March 8, 2013].

Good summary of the life and work of Price for the educated public; first published in 2013 and reprinted on February 7, 2016 in honor of Black History Month. Includes additional information about radio documentary of Terrance McKnight, "The Price of Admission: A Musical Biography of Florence Beatrice Price."

133. Dykema, Dan. "Florence Beatrice Smith Price." *Encyclopedia of Arkansas Music*. Edited by Ali Welky & Mike Keckhaver. Little Rock, Arkansas: Butler Center Books, 2013, pp. 172–73. ISBNs: 9781935106609, 1935106600; 9781935106616, 1935106619.

Basic biography with supplemental list of eight published sources for additional reading.

134. Fuller, Sophie. "Florence Price 1888–1953." *The Pandora Guide to Women Composers: Britain and the United States, 1629-Present*. London: Harper Collins (Pandora), 1994, pp. 254–56. ISBN: 9780044409366, 0044409362.

An intelligent summary of the life and work of Price in a collection covering British and American female composers. Includes appendix that lists publications for additional reading. Entries are alphabetical by name of composer, which essentially precludes consideration of historical connections between composers. Account of musical works in body of each essay.

135. Green, Mildred Denby. *Black Women Composers: A Genesis*. Boston: G.K. Hall (Twayne Publishers), 1983. 171 pp. ISBN: 9780805794502, 0805794506.

See pages 31–46 (Chapter 2: "Florence Price 1888–1953"), pages 145–53 (bibliography), pages 154–67 (catalog of musical works) and page 158 (discography). Presumably influenced by author's dissertation (see next entry).

136. Green, Mildred Denby. "A Study of the Lives and Works of Five Black Women Composers in America." Ph.D. diss., University of Oklahoma, 1975. vii, 323 pp. DDM: 71woGreM; RILM: UM no. 76-15, 803.

The first dissertation involved with the music of Price (although only as one of several composers), foreshadowing others by Carren Moham, Brown, Scott Farah, Linda Holzer, Sarah Peebles, Lisa Lee Sawyer, Teresa Shelton, Bethany Jo Smith and Stephanie White, which are all listed below. Green's work on this dissertation and her subsequent book (see preceding entry) influenced many other scholars.

137. Greeson, James, ed. *The Caged Bird: The Life and Music of Florence B. Price*. [Fayetteville, Arkansas]: University of Arkansas Press, 2015. ISBN: 9781682260067, 1682260062.

Comprises videos, slides and a fifty-seven-minute documentary film. Greeson was the producer, writer and cameraman as well as the editor. Presented at the Gene Siskel Film Center of the Art Institute of Chicago on August 21, 1916. Sponsored by the University of Arkansas, which houses a major repository of

Price's musical manuscripts and other unpublished papers. Copies of this film are in the libraries of the University of Wisconsin at Madison and the University of Illinois at Champaign-Urbana.

138. Jackson, Barbara Garvey. "Florence Price, Composer." *The Black Perspective in Music* 5 (Spring 1977): 30–43.

Relatively early assessment of the music of Price; contemporary with the pioneering research of Mildred Denby Green and Raoul Abdul-Rahim. Jackson's subsequent work in this area included the introductory essay for the first edition of Price's *Five Folksongs in Counterpoint for String Quartet* (see no. 165) and her own edition of Price's choral *Communion Service* (see no. 162).

139. Lynch, Janet Nichols. *Women Music Makers: An Introduction to Women Composers*. New York: Walker, 1992. xiv, 224 pp. ISBN: 9780802781697, 0802781691.

Comprises accounts of ten composers including Fanny Mendelssohn-Hensel, Clara Wieck-Schumann, Ethel Smyth, Amy Beach and Price (her entry covers pp. 110–25). May be suitable for students as well as adult readers.

140. Moham, Carren D. "The Contributions of Four African-American Women Composers to American Art Song." Diss., Ohio State University, 1997. xii, 84 pp.

Comprises chapters covering Price, Bonds, Undine Smith-Moore and Dorothy Rudd-Moore.

141. Morris, Mellasenah. "Florence Smith Price." *Black Women in America*. Edited by Darlene Clark Hine, Rosalyn Terborg-Penn & Elsa Barkley Brown. New York: Oxford University Press, 2005. 2 vols. [xxvii, 1530 pp.] ISBN: 0780926019614, 0926019619.

Listed in the catalog of the Chicago Public Library but could not be located in the stacks.

MUSICO-ANALYTICAL

Analytic Essays and Articles

142. Brown, Rae Linda. "Florence B. Price's Negro Symphony." *Temples for Tomorrow: Looking Back at the Harlem Renaissance*. Edited by Geneviève Fabre & Michel Feith. Bloomington: Indiana University Press, 2001. x, 392 pp. ISBNs: 9780364325366, 0253214254; 9780253328861, 0253328861.

Apostrophizes the *Symphony no. 1*, which became a major factor in Price's growing reputation as a composer in the 1930s in the context of other such works by Still and Dawson in the same period.

143. Brown, Rae Linda. "Selected Orchestral Music of Florence B. Price (1888–1953) in the Context of Her Life and Work." Ph.D. diss., Yale University, 1987. v, 237 pp.

The first of many publications from this scholar specifically devoted to the works of Price—her doctoral dissertation—although she had anticipated this specialty in her catalog of the James Weldon Johnson collection (see no. 117). Comprises six chapters, the first three outlining historical background and the others devoted to *Symphony in e minor*, the *Piano Concerto in One Movement* and the *Symphony in c minor*. Exhaustive analyses of all three works complemented by a bibliography and a list of works in genre sections.

144. Brown, Rae Linda. "The Women's Symphony Orchestra of Chicago and Florence B. Price's Piano Concerto in One Movement." *American Music* 11 (1993): 185–205.

Documentation of early performances of the *Symphony in e minor* and the *Piano Concerto*, which were both performed by the Chicago Symphony Orchestra and subsequently at the World's Fair of 1933. Full analysis of the concerto with extensive musical examples. This is a rare study that gives equal weight to Price as both black and female.

145. Farrah, Scott David. "Signifyin(g): A Semiotic Analysis of Symphonic Worlds by William Grant Still, William Levi Dawson, and Florence B. Price." Ph.D. diss., Florida State University, 2007. xii, 170 pp.

Comparison of the political basis of three symphonies composed by black composers of the early twentieth century: the *Afro-American Symphony* of Still, the *Negro Folk Symphony* of Dawson and the *Symphony in e minor* of Price. Grouping of these works is especially interesting since Price and Still had known each other for many years, and he rendered professional assistance to her on multiple occasions.

146. Holzer, Linda Ruth. "Selected Solo Piano Music of Florence B. Price (1887–1953)." D.M.A. thesis, Florida State University, 1995. vii, 99 pp.

Indexed in *Doctoral Dissertations in Musicology* (DDM-1928) and *RILM* (1995-05848). This thesis is intended as an introduction of the piano music of Price for performers rather than historians.

147. Kazmier, Will. "In Search of Florence Price's Symphony no. 1: Reviving a Prize-Winning Work by a Forgotten African American Female Composer." *Fanfare* 49 (2013): 13–16.

This significant article was published in the alumni magazine of the Northwestern University Bienen School of Music, covering in detail the problems, preparation and performance of the *Symphony no. 1*. Appears to have been the first performance of the symphony in the Chicago area since 1933.

148. Peebles, Sarah Louise. "The Use of the Spiritual in the Piano Works of Two African-American Women Composers—Florence B. Price and Margaret Bonds." D.A. diss., University of Mississippi, 2008. x, 148 leaves.

Comparison of the piano works of the two composers who were friends and colleagues for many years with particular focus on the role of spirituals as the basis of melodic style. The idea of selecting works for piano rather than songs—which would have been rather obvious—or works for chamber ensembles and orchestral music is original.

149. Sawyer, Lisa Lee. "Unpublished Songs of Florence B. Price." D.M.A. thesis, University of Missouri-Kansas City Conservatory of Music, 1990. vi, 360 pp.

Important study of source materials for songs of Price, which, at that time, had never been published (a problem that still exists today). See no. 170 for edition of two songs published for the first time in 1994, which gives credit to Sawyer for the initial discovery.

150. Shelton, Teresa Lorraine. "Idiosyncrasies of Music Narrative: Hypotheses for Further Investigation." Ph.D. diss., Indiana University, 1997. xii, 217 pp.

Analysis of the first movement of Price's *Piano Sonata in e minor* compared with other works in the context of Eero Tarasti's theory of semiotics.

151. Smith, Bethany Jo. "Song to the Dark Virgin: Race and Gender in Five Art Songs of Florence B. Price." M.M. thesis, University of Cincinnati College-Conservatory of Music, 2007. 130 pp.

Compare this analysis with the edition of *Song to the Dark Virgin* included in *New Historical Anthology of Music by Women* (see no. 156). This thesis addresses the basis of the composer's vocal style in more detail than Melissa Blakesly was able to include in the anthology.

152. Southern, Eileen. *The Music of Black America: A History*. New York: W.W. Norton, 1971. xviii, 552 pp. 2nd edition (1983) xx, 602 pp. 3rd edition (1997) xxii, 678 pp. ISBNs: 0393021564 (1971), 0393952797 (1983), 0393038432, 0393971414 (1997).

A separate achievement from Southern's later *Biographical Dictionary of Afro-American and African Musicians* (see above). Documents the African and Afro-American heritage in music in four parts: (1) 1619–1775, (2) 1776–1866, (3) 1867–1919 and (4) 1920 to date of publication. Rather than detail about individuals, author focuses on chronology and typology of the music itself including "popular" as well as "classical" music.

153. Tischler, Alice & Carol Tomasic. *Fifteen Black American Composers: A Bibliography of Their Works*. Detroit: Information Coordinators, 1981. 328 pp.

No specific chapter covering Price, but there is relevant information in the chapter covering her student and friend Bonds. Includes biography, list of musical works (including full publication and performing information) and supplemental bibliography.

154. White, Stephanie Lawrence. "The Piano Music of Florence Beatrice Price: An Examination of Three Characteristic Works." M.A. thesis, Catholic University of America, 1998. 72 pp.

Copy available only at Catholic University of America as the originating institution. Not indexed in *Doctoral Dissertations in Musicology* or abstracted in *RILM*.

155. Wright-Pryor, Barbara. "Florence Price: The Mississippi River." *Chicago Symphony Orchestra Program Notes* 122 (May 9, 11 & 14, 2013): 38–45.

Program notes for the first performance of this major orchestral work of Price by the Chicago Symphony Orchestra, which—as of this date—is not published. Covers not only the music in question but gives a detailed background about the composer's life and career.

Scores and Editions

156. Blakesly, Melissa. "Florence Price (1887–1953)." *New Historical Anthology of Music by Women*. Edited by James R. Briscoe. Bloomington & Indianapolis: Indiana University Press, 2004, pp. 358–64. ISBN: 9780253216830, 0253216834.

New addition to the revised collection first published in 1987 in which Price was not included. Introduction with succinct biography, analysis of Price's musical style and edition of "Song to the Dark Virgin," for voice and piano. See relevant assessment in Smith's thesis (no. 151).

157. *The Florence Price Collection*. Flagstaff, Arizona: William Grant Still Music, 198 [25 pages in various paginations].

Five works for piano and one for organ; reprinted from previous editions by Price's longtime friend and colleague Still:

- *Dances in the Canebrakes*
- *In Quiet Mood* [organ]
- *The Old Boatman*
- *Cotton Dance*
- *Ticklin' Toes*
- *Levee Dance*

Previous publishers of these works include Affiliated Musicians (see no. 167), Clayton F. Summy and Theodore Presser (see no. 169). See also next entry in which Calvert Johnson, the editor of Price's organ works, included *In Quiet Mood*, the only work in this compendium for organ rather than piano. The score of *Dances in the Canebrakes* is preceded by an illustration, and that entry bears faint pencil marks—probably from Still—planning orchestration that was published (in an edition by Michael Kibbe) in 1997.

158. Johnson, Calvert, ed. *Music of Florence Beatrice Price*. Fayetteville, Arkansas: ClarNan Editions, 1993-1996. 4 vols.

> Vol. 1: *Suite no. 1 for Organ*. xxxv, 25 pp.
> Vol. 2: *Short Organ Works*. xli, 32 pp. [*Adoratio,. Allegretto, Festal March, The Hour Glass (=Sandman), In Quiet Mood (=Impromptu), Little Melody. Offertory, A Pleasant Thought,* and *Retrospection (=An Elf on a Moonbeam)*
> Vol. 3: *Variations on Folksong "Peter, Go Ring dem Bells" for Organ*. xxi, 20 pp.
> Vol. 4: *First Sonata for Organ*. xxxv, 37 pp.

A rare publication of the works of Price for organ, which constitutes a small but important part of her work. Editor is professional organist experienced with performance of Price's work.

159. Nyaho, William Chapman, ed. *Piano Music of Africa and the African Diaspora*. New York: Oxford University Press, 2007-2008. 5 vols.

Two works by Price are included in this compendium for piano: *Ticklin' Toes* (vol. 1, pp. 15-17) and *Silk Hat and Walking Cane* (vol. 2, pp. 24-28). Both of these works are listed below (no. 167 and no. 169); in their early editions during the composer's lifetime.

160. Price, Florence. "The Rose." *The Second Assembled Book of Pieces We Like to Play*. Edited by Gail Martin Haake, Charles J. Haake & Osbourne McConathy. New York: Carl Fischer, 1936. 32 pp.

The last of fourteen pieces by various composers (pp. 30-32).

161. Price, Florence. "The Gnat and the Bee." *The Third Assembled Book of Pieces We Like to Play*. Edited by Gail Martin Haake, Charles J. Haake & Osbourne McConathy. New York: Carl Fischer, 1934. 32 pp.

The eighth of twelve pieces by various composers (pp. 21-23).

The two books above are volumes of music for children published in the 1930s as a progressive course of piano studies in which the publisher Carl Fischer (New York and Chicago) was involved for many years. The editors chose a wide selection of works by many composers. As Price was actively teaching piano during the period when these books were published, they were probably composed for her own students.

162. Price, Florence. *Communion Service in F for SATB Choir and Organ*. Edited by Barbara Garvey Jackson. Fayetteville, Arkansas: ClarNan Editions, 2015. 41 pp.

The sections (all in English) comprise:

- *Kyrie eleison*
- *Before the Gospel/After the Gospel*

- *Credo*
- *Sursum Corda*
- *Sanctus*
- *Benedictus*
- *Agnus Dei*
- *Gloria in Excelsis*

Akin to the four volumes of organ works from the same publisher (1993–96), this work is little known in spite of the fact that Price was an experienced church organist.

163. Price, Florence. "The Heart of a Woman" and "The Glory of the Day Was in Her Face." *Women Composers: Music Through the Ages, Vol. 7: Composers Born 1800–1899, Vocal Music*. Edited by Rae Linda Brown. Farmington Hills, Michigan: G.K. Hall/Gale Group, 2003, pp. 738–52. ISBN: 9780783881942, 0783881940.

Exhaustive introduction to the life and works of the composer (by Brown) with a classified list of the composer's works, bibliography, discography and edition of the above two songs, which were published here for the first time.

164. Price, Florence. *44 Art Songs and Spirituals*. Edited by Richard Heard. Fayetteville, Arkansas: ClarNan Editions, 2015. x, 173 pp.

Collection of songs with account of the composer's life and an accompanying CD.

165. Price, Florence. "Five Folksongs in Counterpoint for String Quartet." *Women Composers: Music Through the Ages, Vol. 8: Composers Born 1800–1899: Large and Small Instrumental Ensembles*. Co-edited by Barbara Garvey Jackson (essay), Rae Linda Brown (edition of score) & Martha Furman Schleifer (thematic analysis). Farmington Hills, Michigan: G.K. Hall/Gale Group, 2006, pp. 457–92. ISBN: 9780783881935, 0783881932.

In contrast with the previous volume of this anthology (see no. 163), this volume is devoted to twenty works for instrumental ensembles. Price is in good company with such other composers as Ethel Smyth and Amy Beach. The introductory materials before the score of the quartet (comprising essay, endnotes, select list of works, bibliography and discography) are abbreviated compared with the long introduction to the vocal works in vol. 7. The five folk songs forming the basis of this chamber work are:

- *Calvary*
- *Clementine*
- *Drink to Me Only With Thine Eyes*
- *Shortnin' Bread*
- *Swing Low, Sweet Chariot*

166. Price, Florence. *Sonata in e minor for Piano.* Edited by Rae Linda Brown. New York: G. Schirmer [distributed by Milwaukee: Hal Leonard Corp.], 1997. [ii], 35 pp. ISBN: 9780793551309, 0793551307.

Two preliminary pages devoted to a brief biography of the composer and an analysis of the sonata. Editor notes that this work dates from 1932 but does not offer information about publication during the composer's lifetime. Comprises four movements:

- *Andante.Allegretto.Tempo I.Presto*
- *Andante. Piu Mosso [Rondo]*
- *Scherzo*
- *Allegro.Cantabile Maestoso.Allegro.Allegro.Andantino.Allegro.Andantino. Presto*

167. Price, Florence. *Dances in the Canebrakes.* Los Angeles: Affiliated Musicians, 1953. 13 pp. [Original version for piano.] Orchestral version by William Grant Still (edited by Michael Kibbe) [Flagstaff, Arizona]: William Grant Still Music, 1997. 39 pp.

Comprises "Nimble Feet," "Tropical Noon" and "Silk Hat and Walking Cane." The complement in the orchestral version comprises two flutes, two clarinets, bassoon, two horns, two trumpets, timpani, percussion and strings.

168. Price, Florence. *Symphonies 1 and 3.* Coedited by Rae Linda Brown & Wayne Shirley. Middleton, Wisconsin: A-R Editions, 2008. lii, [3], 296 pp. ISBN: 9780895796387, 0895796384.

Comprises orchestral scores of the two symphonies (the *Symphony no. 2* does not appear to have survived), with an exhaustive introductory essay, critical notes for each of the two symphonies, list of sources and a bibliography of relevant literature. One of several scores of works by Price (see also organ and choral scores from ClarNan listed above) that stand as models for all future publications of Price's music.

169. Price, Florence. *Ticklin' Toes, from Three Little Negro Dances.* Bryn Mawr, Pennsylvania: Theodore Presser, 1933. 5 pp.

This is the last of the three dances; the others are *Rabbit Foot* and *Hoe Cake*. All three works were published in an arrangement for band by Erik W.G. Leidzen (Philadelphia: Theodore Presser, 1939). There is also an undated version for orchestra [two flutes, two clarinets, one bassoon, two horns, two trumpets, timpani, percussion and strings]. 13 & 27 leaves in manuscript.

170. Price, Florence. *Two Songs.* San Antonio, Texas: Southern Music Company, 1994. 7 pp.

See no. 149 for relevant thesis by Lisa Lee Sawyer whose research on unpublished songs of Price was a direct precursor of this edition. Comprises "Feet o'Jesus" (with a text by Langston Hughes) and "Trouble Done Come My Way" (for which Price herself wrote the text as well as the music).

171. Taylor, Vivian, ed. *Art Songs and Spirituals by African-American Women Composers.* Bryn Mawr, Pennsylvania: Hildegard Publishing Company, 1995. vi, 88 pp.

This collection comprises works of Price, Bonds, Julia Perry, Undine Smith-Moore and Betty Jackson-King. Four of the nineteen works are by Price:

- *My Dream*
- *Song to the Dark Virgin*
- *Night*
- *My Soul's Been Anchored in the Lord*

172. Walker-Hill, Helen & Montague Ring, eds. *Black Women Composers: A Century of Piano Music, 1893–1990.* Bryn Mawr, Pennsylvania: Hildegard Publishing Company, 1992. 83 pp.

This collection and the preceding one were published by Hildegard Publishing, which has been a pioneer in specialization of music by female composers. The two books are differentiated only by genres. Price's *Fantasie Negre* (1929) (which is known as the basis of a ballet choreographed by Katherine Dunham) is included on pp. 25–35 of this volume. Walker-Hill subsequently contributed *From Spirituals to Symphonies: African-American Women Composers and Their Music* (Westport, Connecticut: Greenwood Press, 2002; Urbana, Illinois: University of Illinois Press, 2007), which fleshed out these editions with historical background.

IV

María Teresa Prieto Fernández de la Llana

REFERENCE BOOKS

173. Carredano, Consuelo. *Ediciones Méxicanas de Música: Historia y Catálogo.* México D.F.: CENDIM, 1994. 413 pp. ISBN: 9789682975943, 9782975948.

   A significant reference covering the history of the publishing house in Mexico City, which was responsible for the publication of many musical works of María Teresa Prieto. Documents history of the publisher and lists all publications.

174. Casares Rodicio, Emilio, director y coordinador general. *Diccionario de la Música Española e Hispanoamericana.* Directores adjuntos, José López-Calo y Ismael Fernández de la Cuesta. Secretaria Técnica, María Luz González Peña. Madrid: Sociedad General de Autores y Editores, 1999–2002. 10 vols. ISBN: 9788480483117.

   See vol. 8, pages 941–44 for articles about Prieto, her brother Carlos and other musical specialists in the family including the conductor Carlos Miguel Prieto.

175. Chase, Gilbert. *Guide to Latin American Music.* Washington, DC: Library of Congress, 1945. 274 pp. 2nd edition: *A Guide to the Music of Latin America.* Washington, DC: Pan American Union, 1962. xi, 411 pp.

   Detailed introduction to music of Mexico and Latin America; much enlarged in the second edition. Gilbert Chase, having been born in Havana, Cuba and having served in the diplomatic service in countries including Peru and Argentina, was indefatigable in his ethno-musicological research, which provided a basis for the developing work of many composers including the Mexicans with whom Prieto studied in the 1930s and 1940s.

176. *Compositores de America: Datos Biograficos y Catalogos de sus Obras/Composers of the Americas: Biographical Data and Catalogs of Their Works.* Washington, DC: Pan American Union Music Section, 1955–1993. 20 vols. [Periodical]

   No entry covering Prieto, but articles about her teachers Manuel Ponce (vol. 1, pp. 60–70) and Rodolfo Halffter (vol. 2, pp. 83–89) include related subject matter.

177. Draayer, Suzanne Rhodes. *Art Song Composers of Spain: An Encyclopedia.* Lanham, Maryland: Scarecrow Press, 2009. xxvii, 518 pp. ISBNs: 9780810863620, 0810863626; 9780810867192, 0810867192.

   No specific reference to Prieto, but information about the brothers Ernesto and Halffter who, like Prieto, emigrated to Mexico (Halffter was among her teachers) helps to offer a rounded picture of the circumstances in which her career was initiated.

178. Pena, Joaquin. *Diccionario de la Música Labor.* Iniciado por Joaquin Pena, continuado por Higinio Anglés, con la colaboracion de Miguel Querol y otros distinguidos musicólogos españoles extrajanos. Barcelona: Labor, 1954. 2 vols. [x], 2318 pp.

   An early bio-bibliography equivalent to Hugo Riemann's *Musiklexikon*; developed into a separate entity with new materials from Spanish and Latin American scholars.

179. Ricart Matas, José. *Diccionario Biográfico de la Música.* 2nd edition. Barcelona: Iberia, 1966. 1143 pp.

   Listed in the catalog of the Chicago Public Library but could not be located in the stacks.

180. Schleifer, Martha Furman & Galván, Gary, eds. *Latin American Classical Composers: A Biographical Dictionary.* 3rd edition. Lanham, [Maryland]: Rowman & Littlefield, 2016. xxvii, 735 pp. ISBN: 9780810888708, 081088870X.

   Good summary of Prieto's life and work but only limited bibliography listing additional sources.

181. Spiess, Lincoln Bunce. *An Introduction to Certain Mexican Musical Archives.* Detroit: Information Coordinators, 1969. 84, [99] pp.

   Relatively early catalog of archival materials that were little known outside Mexico. Lincoln Bunce Spiess was a specialist in music of Mexico and the American Southwest from the Renaissance forward; this listing of sources is significant because it demonstrated what could be accomplished in an assessment of the long history of music in Mexico, although it did not focus on sources from the work of Prieto and other Mexican composers of the twentieth century.

HISTORICAL CONTEXT

182. Baqueiro Fóster, Gerónimo. *La Música en el Periodo Independiente*. Historia de la Música en México, 3. México City: Departamento de Música/NBA/SEP, 1964.

    Installment in a multivolume history of music in Mexico, this volume covering the period from the nineteenth to the mid-late twentieth century. Published at a time when Prieto was particularly active among Mexican composers including her teachers Ponce, Carlos Chavez and Halffter. Geronimo Baqueiro Fóster was a professional who contributed to many publications about Mexican music.

183. Godoy, Susan. "Mexican Music from 1920 to 1953." Ph.D. diss., Radcliffe College, 1961. Vol. 1: 463 pp. Vols. 2–3: 707 pp. music.

    Listed in *Doctoral Dissertations in Musicology* (DDS-8885). One of the first doctoral dissertations in English on the subject of music in Mexico, including detailed commentary preceding extensive musical examples. Covers the period when Prieto came to live in Mexico City and began to develop her career as a composer.

184. Hague, Eleanor. *Latin American Music: Past and Present*. Santa Ana, California: Fine Arts Press, 1934. 98 pp.

    Very early, concise introduction to the music of many Spanish-speaking countries in the New World, including Mexico. Predates the work of Spiess, Chase, Orin Lincoln Igou and other scholars from the United States and Mexico. This offers a view of musical activity only a few years before Prieto made her home in Mexico.

185. Igou, Orin Lincoln. "Contemporary Symphonic Activity in Mexico with Special Regard to Carlos Chavez and Silvestre Revueltas." Ph.D. diss., Northwestern University, 1946. 593 pp.

    Listed in *Doctoral Dissertations in Musicology* (DDM-9288). Early dissertation devoted to the work of the leading Mexican composers Chavez and Silvestre Revueltas. Chavez was one of Prieto's teachers. Revueltas, while not in a position to be involved with her education after her emigration to Mexico, was three years younger than Prieto, and—like her—gained valuable education in the United States while being involved in the cause of Mexican nationalist music.

186. Marco, Tomás. *Historia de la Música Española*. 3rd edition. Madrid: Alianza, 1993. 364 pp. ISBN: 9788420685069, 8420685062.

    Detailed coverage of the musical history of Spain in twenty-three chapters divided into two halves. Chapter 4, "Independientes," of Part II, includes a detailed assessment of the compositions of Prieto, a rare recognition of the work of Spanish composers who lived and worked in the New World.

187. Mayer-Serra, Otto. *Música y Músicos de Latinoamérica*. Mexico: Editorial Atlante, 1947. 2 vols. [1134 pp.]

Summary of Prieto's life (vol. 2, pp. 794–95), with a photograph of her, and a select list of works with dates, including:

- *Oración de Quietud* (1939) [soprano and orchestra]
- *Impresión Sinfónica* (1940) [piano and orchestra]
- *Excelsitud* (1941) [chorus and orchestra]
- *Sinfonia Asturiana* (1942) [orchestra]

This is supplemental information to be combined with the select list of scores found below (see nos. 203–218).

188. Mendoza, Vicente T. *La Canción Méxicana: Ensayo de Clasificación y Antología*. México [City]: Universidad Nacional, 1961. 671 pp. 2nd edition: México [City]: Fondo de Cultura Económico, 1982. 637 pp.

Exhaustive study of the history of Mexican songs, comprising introduction and many examples that offer a historical context to the work of Prieto and other composers influenced by indigenous music in their own compositions. Revised edition of 1982 was published under government auspices, which suggests the cultural importance of this research.

189. Moreno Rivas, Yolanda. *La Composición en México en el Siglo XX*. Presentación, Luis Ignacio Helguera. México, D.F.: Consejo Nacional para la Cultura y las Artes, 1994. 383 pp. ISBN: 9682955637, 9682961637.

No references to Prieto, but historical context provided by assessment of her teachers (Ponce, Chavez and Halffter). Covers the period 1940–1991. Supplemented by a useful bibliography.

190. Pulido, Esperanza. *La Mujer Méxicana en la Música: (Hasta la Tercera Década del Siglo XX*. México: Ediciones de la Revista Bellas Artes, 1958. 126 pp.

A relatively early contribution to studies of musical typologies in Mexico, comprising ten chapters more or less chronologically ordered. Unusual to see a book from that time period specifically devoted to female musicians. Chapters 9 (pp. 87–106) and 10 (pp. 107–26) cover the time period in which Prieto lived, studied and established her career in Mexico; she is noted in the last pages of the book.

191. Zaimont, Judith Lang, ed. *The Musical Woman: An International Perspective*. Vol. II (1984–1985). Westport, Connecticut: Greenwood Press, 1987. xxv, 557 pp. ISBN: 9780313235887, 0313235880.

See relevant article by Esperanza Pulido, "National Survey: Mexico's Women Musicians," and compare it with related assessment in Spanish by same author cited in preceding entry.

BIOGRAPHICAL

192. Alvarez, Leticia. "Cultura Recopita la Obra de la Compositora Teresa Prieto: La OSPA Revivirá la Música de la Autora Ovetense Exiliada en México."

El Comercio Es. [www.elcomercio.es/gijon/20070930/sociedad/cultura-recopila-obra-compositora-20070930].

Popular periodical accessible online, with a concise report of the life and work of Prieto including suggestion of support for her remarkable career as an exile in Mexico, a controversial subject between Mexican and Spanish scholars.

193. Barce, Ramón. "María Teresa Prieto: Vida y Obra." *Ritmo*. (October 1986): 97.

One-page summary of Prieto's life and a selected list of her works, as well as a photograph. Part of a series "Músicos del Siglo XX," which appears in every monthly issue. Essay argues for Prieto as Spanish rather than Mexican, a controversial subject.

194. Campos Fonseca, Susan. "Between Left-Led Republic and Falangism? Spanish Women Composers, A Critical Equation." 20 pp. Found in the following websites:

www.academia.edu/724103
www.researchgate.net/publication/265574125_Between_Left_Led
http://cilam.ucr.edu/diagonal/issues/2011/Campos.pdf

Rare contribution in English to the literature about Prieto and other female composers in the Spanish-speaking countries during the twentieth century. Serious consideration—well documented with published references—about the historical position of Prieto and others who emigrated from Spain to Mexico; documents controversy about whether such composers should be considered exiles, which informs rival claims to Prieto from Spanish and Mexican musicologists, most notably affecting publication and performance of her music.

195. Casares Rodicio, Emilio. "La Compositora María Teresa Prieto: Del Postromanticismo al Estructuralismo Dodecafónico." *Boletín del Instituto de Estudios Asturianos*, no. 95 (1978): 715–53.

Detailed study of the work of Prieto, suggesting an analytical assessment of her compositional style, which apparently progressed from derivative beginnings based on post-romanticism that she might have learned in her early education in Oviedo and Madrid, to twelve-tone style based on Arnold Schoenberg and his students. Questions might be raised with respect to the composer's use of forms based on music as early as Johann Sebastian Bach and the influence of Darius Milhaud, with whom she studied in 1946–1947.

196. Casares Rodicio, Emilio. "Prieto, María Teresa." *Norton/Grove Dictionary of Women Composers*, pp. 375–76.

This functions as a summary of the same author's long article on the subject of Prieto from 1978 (see preceding entry). There is no existing entry covering this composer in the 1980 edition of *The New Grove Dictionary of Music and Musicians*, the basis for this and other *Grove Dictionaries* addressing specialized subject matter.

197. Lynn, Jennifer Kaye. "María Teresa Prieto: A Biography and a Discussion of *Seis Melodias*." M.F.A. thesis, Mills College, 1997. 33 pp.

Rare study of the life of Prieto, with the choice of *Seis Melodias* (published by G. Schirmer in 1942) as an example of the composer's work. This thesis was submitted at Mills College, where Prieto herself had studied with Milhaud in 1946–1947. See also no. 213 for the published score, which Prieto herself may have brought with her when she attended Milhaud's classes.

198. *Mujeres de Asturias: La Mujer en la Música de Concierto y Composición.* Gijón, Asturias [Spain]: Ediciones Mases, 1988. 313 pp. ISBN: 9788486328559, 8486328551.

See http://mujeresinstrumentitas.blogspot.com/2008/11/maria-teresa-composicion.html, which is credited to Juan Santana, for related information.

199. Prieto, María Teresa. *Pirulin: Narración Verídica.* [True Narration.] México: Rómulus, 1962. 20 pp.

"Narrativa Mexicana." Prieto was a writer as well as a composer (she was known to write some of the texts she set in her vocal works); this short book suggests a *novella* based on personal experiences.

200. Pulido, Esperanza. "Mexican Women in Music." *Latin American Music Review / Revista de Música Latinoamericana.* 4 (Spring/Summer 1983): 120–31.

Published shortly after the death of Prieto, this short account of Mexican women in music is a basis for additional search in the research of Leticia Alvarez and Ramon Barce (see nos. 192–93) and Pablo J. Vayón (see no. 202).

201. Sordo Sodi, Carmen. "Compositoras Méxicanos de Música Comercial." *Heterofinia.* 15 (1982): 16–20.

Account of public music by female Mexican composers.

202. Vayón, Pablo J. "Memoria de una Exiliada." *Diario de Sevilla el Sábado* (14 de Junio de 2008). [www.diariodesevilla.es/article/ocio/155309/memoria/una/exiliada/html].

Concise account of the life of Prieto, with significant information about her major compositions, especially those for orchestra. Published in Spain but offers more positive recognition of the composer's work in Mexico than is usually found in publications from Spanish scholars.

MUSICO-ANALYTICAL

Scores and Editions

203. Prieto, María Teresa. *Adagio y Fuga para Cello y Orquesta.* 1947–48. Photocopy of the manuscript for orchestra at University of North Carolina at Greensboro Library [Special Collections Eisenberg Box 6–11]. 51 pp.

Adagio y Fuga para Cello y Piano. México, D.F.: Ediciones Méxicanas de Música, 1953. 13 pp. This is the version for cello solo with piano in lieu of orchestra.

A slow prelude followed by a multi-sectional fugue, in both of which the soloist and the pianist (or orchestra) are equal partners. Considered to be influenced by comparable works of Bach.

204. Prieto, María Teresa. *Allegro Moderato.* For orchestra.

Photocopy of the holograph at the Indiana University Library. 41 pp. Not published as of this writing.

205. Prieto, María Teresa. *Ave Maria para Canto y Organo o Piano.* México, D.F.: Ediciones Méxicanas de Música, 1966. 7 pp.

Short liturgical work for unspecified solo voice and organ. Prelude, interlude and postlude demanding for organist, although the specified tempo is primarily *andante*. Vocal sections simple and rather tonal, organ line following the voice. May have been modeled on the style of Bach cantatas.

206. Prieto, María Teresa. *Canciones Modales: Para Canto y Piano.* México, D.F.: Ediciones Méxicanas de Música, 1963. 18 pp.

Six songs for voice and piano, each in a different modal center based on medieval/Renaissance theories, comprising the following:

- *Si Ves el Ciervo Herido*
- *Sonatina*
- *De Extremadura a Leon*
- *Esta Verde Hierba*
- *Cristo en la Tarde*
- *Quien Dijo Acaso*

207. Prieto, María Teresa. *Chichen Itza.* Copy of manuscript score of tone poem for orchestra, depicting famous geographical site in Mexico (1944).

Orchestral complement: Two flutes/piccolo, two oboes/English horn, two clarinets/bass clarinet, two bassoons, four horns, two trumpets, three trombones, tuba, timpani, percussion, harp and strings.

208. Prieto, María Teresa. *Cuarteto Modal para Instrumentos de Arco.* México, D.F.: Ediciones Méxicanas de Música, 1959. 33 pp.

Four-movement string quartet; influenced partly by works in this form from the Classical period to the twentieth century, partly by the tonal basis of music of the Common Practice period, with which the composer was surely familiar. Each movement is in a different mode:

- *[Dorico] Adagio. Allegro. Adagio. Allegro. Adagio*
- *[Lidio] "Scherzo Allegretto"*
- *[Eólico] "Andante Espressivo"*
- *[Jónico] Fuga. Allegretto non troppo*

209. Prieto, María Teresa. *Cuatro Canciones para Canto y Piano*. México, D.F.: Ediciones Méxicanas de Música, 1971, 1990. 20 pp.

    This collection comprises the following songs for voice and piano:
    - *Dios de Otorgó la Gracia*
    - *Canzón da Noite do, Aflador*
    - *Cantiga*
    - *Oración de Quietud. Poema Sinfonico*

    The last song is much longer than any of the first three. Two of the four texts were from Prieto herself.

210. Prieto, María Teresa. *Música Sinfonica*. Edited by José Luis Temes. [Oviedo]: Gobierno del Principado de Asturias, Consejeria de Cultura, Comunicación Social y Turismo, 2007. 213 pp.

    This is a critical edition of the following works for orchestra, the first such publication in Spain since almost all scores published in the composer's lifetime were published in Mexico and the United States.
    - *Impresión Sinfonica para piano y orquesta*
    - *Cuadros de la Naturaleza*
    - *Preludio "Asturias"*
    - *Il Valle México, poema sinfonico*
    - *Tema Variado y Fuga, en Estilo Dodecafónico* [See no. 218 for a copy of the manuscript]
    - *Sonata Modal para Violonchelo y Orquesta*

211. Prieto, María Teresa. *Odas Celestes: Para Canto y Piano*. México, D.F.: Ediciones Méxicanas de Música, 1952. 18 pp.

    Comprises five songs, most in Spanish (the text of the third is by Prieto herself) and the last in French:
    - *Oda Celeste*
    - *Cantad. Pajaros*
    - *Mirando las Altas Cumbres*
    - *Le Colibri*
    - *Les Peupliers de Kéranroux*

212. Prieto, María Teresa. *"Palo Verde": Suite de Ballet en 5 Movimientos*. 1967. 130 pp. Photocopy of the manuscript orchestral score.

    This suite from a ballet (an unusual form for this composer) comprises five movements:
    - *Obertura*
    - *Fuga*
    - *Scherzino*
    - *Interludio*
    - *Finale*

Comprises the following orchestral complement: two flutes/piccolo, two oboes/English horn, two clarinets/bass clarinet, two bassoons, four horns, two trumpets, three trombones, timpani, percussion, harp and strings.

213. Prieto, María Teresa. *Seis Melodias para Canto y Piano*. New York: Schirmer, 1942. 23 pp.

    This was an early publication from the period when the composer was studying with Halffter, Ponce and Chavez in Mexico City. Compare the score with the M.F.A. thesis of Jennifer Kaye Lynn at Mills College (see no. 197), which may have been based on a copy of this edition brought to that institution by the composer when she studied with Milhaud in 1946-47.

214. Prieto, María Teresa. *Sinfonia Breve*. 1945. Photocopy of the manuscript orchestral score. 91 pp., comprising three movements:

    - *Allegro moderato*
    - *Andante Espressivo*
    - *Allegro*

    This is considered the composer's first symphony. It requires the following orchestral complement: two flutes/piccolo, two oboes/English horn, two clarinets/bass clarinet, two bassoons, four horns, two trumpets, three trombones, tuba, triangle, celesta and strings.

215. Prieto, María Teresa. *Sinfonia Cantabile*. 1954. Photocopy of the manuscript orchestral score. 99 pp. The four movements comprise:

    - *Adagio. Allegro*
    - *Andante*
    - *Tempo di Valse*
    - *Rondo. Allegro*

    This is the composer's second symphony, which requires the following orchestral complement: two flutes/piccolo, two oboes/English horn, two clarinets/bass clarinet, two bassoons, four horns, two trumpets, three trombones, tuba, timpani, triangle, harp and strings. In form, it shows the influence of the classical symphony.

216. Prieto, María Teresa. *Symphony no. 3 "Sinfonia de la Danza Prima"*. 1955. Photocopy of the manuscript orchestral score. 144 pp. Comprises three movements:

    - *Fuga*
    - *Scherzo*
    - *Allegro*

    This work requires the following orchestral complement: four flutes, two piccolos, two oboes/English horn, two clarinets/bass clarinet, two bassoons, four horns, two trumpets, three trombones, tuba, timpani, percussion and strings.

217. Prieto, María Teresa. *24 Variaciones para Piano*. México, D.F.: Ediciones Méxicanas de Música, 1964. 30 pp.

Divided into two halves, each consisting of a theme and twelve variations. Part One, *12 Variaciones Tonales*, preceded by the theme *Andante*; the last variation is a fugue. Part II is titled *12 Variaciones Seriales*. This formal arrangement suggests the influence of Bach and Hindemith as keyboard contrapuntists.

218. Prieto, María Teresa. *Tema Variado y Fuga Dodecafonicos.* 1965. Photocopy of the manuscript orchestral score at Indiana University Library. 41 & 35 pp., comprising the following orchestral complement: two flutes/piccolo, two oboes/English horn, two clarinets/bass clarinet, two bassoons/contrabassoon, four horns, two trumpets, three trombones, tuba, timpani, piano and strings.

Compare with no. 210, which included the published score of this work among other orchestral works.

V
Yuliya Lazarevna Veysberg

REFERENCE BOOKS

219.   Bernandt, Grigoriy Borisovich & Dolzhanskii, Aleksandr Naumovich, comps. *Sovetskie Kompozitory: Kratkii Biograficheskii Spravochnik.* [Soviet Composers: Brief Biographical Guide] Moskva: Sovetskii Kompozitor, 1957. 695 pp.

   Succinct descriptions of composers (Yuliya Veysberg is covered on pp. 106–07) with detailed listing of the composer's works.

220.   Branover, Herman, ed. *Rossiiskaia Evreiskaia Entsiklopediia.* Moskva: Rossiiskaia Akademiia estestvennykh nauk: Rossiiskoizrail'skii entsiklopedicheskii tsentr "EPOS," 1994–2011. 7 vols.

   Encyclopedia of Russian Jews, complemented by an alphabetical list of names, dates and places translated into English by Josif and Vitaly Charny [http://jewishgen.org/belarus/rje_r.html]. Veysberg is listed as no. 1136 in the "V" section. As the first three volumes of the book are devoted to biographical articles, Veysberg should be found in vol. 3. ISBNs: 9789652930330, 9652930334; 9789652930408, 9652930407; 9789652930514, 9652930512.

221.   Hofmeister, Friedrich. *Verzeichnis der in Deutschland seit 1868 erschienenen Werke russischer Komponisten.* Leipzig: Druck der Buchdruckerei Frankenstein, 1949. 253 pp.

   Entries alphabetized by names of composers in German or Germanized Russian. The book covers Russian music published by German music firms 1868–1945. Listings include places and names of publishers but no dates. Composers include Veysberg ("Julie Weissberg") and Mikhail Fabianovich Gnesin among many famous names. Published in East Germany after World War II, suggesting political motivation.

222. Hundert, Gershon David, editor in chief. *The YIVO Encyclopedia of Jews in Eastern Europe*. New Haven, [Connecticut]: Yale University Press, 2008. 2 vols. ISBN: 9780300119039, 0300119038.

This book is a valuable basis for research into many aspects of the lives of Jews in Eastern Europe, including music in the Russian orbit. While there is no biographical article related to Veysberg, the following articles in vol. 2 provide relevant background: "Music" (pp. 1219–37), comprising sections by Mark Slobin, Judit Frigyesi, Walter Zev Feldman, James Loeffler and Marion Jacobson; "Musical Education and Musical Societies" (pp. 1237–40) by Jeffrey Veidlinger.

223. Ilyinsky, Aleksandr Aleksandrovich. *Biografii Kompozitorov s XIX-XX vek*. [Russian Composers of the 19th–20th Centuries] Moskva: K.A. Durnovo, 1901–1904. 4 vols. including index.

A little premature to provide useful documentation of Veysberg and other Jewish students studying in St. Petersburg, but good background that helps by providing historical perspective for their work in the next two decades.

224. Jaffé, Daniel. *Historical Dictionary of Russian Music*. Lanham, Maryland: Scarecrow Press, 2012. xxxviii, 419 pp. ISBN: 9780810853119, 0810853116.

This book comprises a chronology (5500 BC–2011 AD), an introduction and an extensive bibliography, supplementing the main body of alphabetized articles. Veysberg is not specifically included, but the bibliography (pp. 349–417) deserves careful study for leads to other sources.

225. Katzenelson, Lev Izrailevich; Günzberg, David; Dubnow, Simon; & Harkavy, Albert, eds. *Evreiskaya Entsiklopediya*. St. Petersburg: Brokgauz-Efron, [1906–1913]. 16 vols.

See article "Society for Jewish Folksong," vol. 11, columns 923ff.

226. Keldysh, Iurii Vsevolodovich; Shteinpress, Boris Solomonovich; & Iampolskii, Izrail Markovich, eds. *Entsiklopedicheskii Muzykal'nyi Slovar'*. Moskva: Gos. Nauch izdatel'stvo "Bolshaia Sovetskaia Entsiklopediia," 1959, 2nd edition 1966. 326 pp.

Alphabetical dictionary of short articles covering people, places and subjects. No entry about Veysberg in first edition, but she was added in the second edition (p. 80). Also, article about her husband in both editions.

227. *Letopis' Muzykal'noi Literatury: Organ Gosudarstvennoi Bibliografii SSSR*. [Chronicle of Musical Literature: Organ of National Bibliography of the USSR] Moskva: Izdatel'stvo Vsesoiuznoi Knizhnoi Palaty, 1931–present.

Quarterly bibliography of scores and editions. Best used in conjunction with single-volume catalog from Friedrich Hofmeister in East Germany specializing in Russian music published in Germany from the nineteenth century through World War II (see no. 221).

228. Riemann, Hugo. *Muzykal'nyi Slovar'*. [Musical Lexicon] Translated from the German original by Joel Engel. Moskva: P. Jurgenson, 1901–1904. 1531 pp.

Russian version of Hugo Riemann's *Musiklexikon*; translated into Russian and augmented with many additions on Russian subjects that Riemann himself had not included. A little too early for inclusion of Veysberg and others of her generation, but Joel Engel provided solid historical context.

229. Sendrey, Alfred. *Bibliography of Jewish Music*. New York: Columbia University Press, 1951. xli, 404 pp.

Exhaustive bibliography comprising books; articles and essays; musical scores; and manuscripts, divided into two sections—the first half devoted to secondary literature and the second to musical scores. Most of the entries include complete publication information and locations indicated by sigla. Even after the elapse of many years since this book was published, the wealth of information is unparalleled. Many items document the work of Russian Jewish composers based in St. Petersburg, Moscow and other centers of education and publication.

230. Soroker, Iakov L'vovich. *Rossiiskie Muzykanty, Evrei: Bio-Bibliograficheskii Leksikon*. [Russian Jewish Musicians: Bio-Bibliographical Lexicon] Jerusalem: Y[akov] Soroker, 1992. 2 vols.

Published by the author in Israel, but in Russian rather than Hebrew. Useful for basis of research rather than commentary.

HISTORICAL CONTEXT

231. Akulova, L.V. *Muzyka v Russkoi Kulture*. Vladimir [Russia]: Izdatel'stvo Iarosvet, 2002. 323 pp.

Chapters 9–12 include discussion of the Russian nationalist composers in cultural context, without musical examples or other illustrative materials.

232. Ansky, Shlomo [*nom de plume* of Shmuel Rapaport]. *Dos Yidishe Etnografishe Program*. Petrograd: Evreiskaia etnograficheskaia ekspeditsiia imeni Barona G.O. Gintsburga, 1914. 120 leaves.

The name Shlomo Ansky as playwright and ethnographic researcher in the late Russian Empire is well known among historians of Jewish music, since the expeditions into far-flung parts of the Empire were specifically for the purpose of collecting Jewish music regardless of where it was found. The work of Engel during these expeditions influenced other Jewish composers (and possibly some Russian ones) to continue and extend such research after the Revolution and the establishment of the Soviet Union.

233. Bacher, Wilhelm. "Ein hebräisches Lied zu Simchat-Thora aus Buchara und Jemen." *Mitteilungen der Gesellschaft für Jüdische Volkskunde* 4 (1901): 68–75, 111–13.

Unusually detailed report documenting ethno-musicological research of religious music in the Jewish communities of Bukhara and Yemen—in German—at the beginning of the twentieth century. This predates similar research by Ansky (see preceding entry), Engel and other Jewish scholars, which formed the basis for Jewish music as a basis for education at the major conservatories in the Russian Empire.

234. Bayer, Bathja. "Society for Jewish Folk Music." *Encyclopedia Judaica*. 2nd edition. New York: Gale Group, 2008, vol. 18, p. 725.

Brief summary of the history and work of the Society for Jewish Folk Music, which was active in St. Petersburg, Moscow and other cities during the time period 1908–1918, when it was terminated after the Russian Revolution.

235. Boelza, Igor F. *Handbook of Soviet Musicians*. London: Pilot Press, 1944. Reprinted St. Clair Shores, Michigan: Scholarly Press, 1972. xiv, 101 pp.

Includes chapters covering Reinhold Gliere, Gnesin, Mikhail Ippolitov-Ivanov, Aram Khachaturyan, Maximilian Steinberg and Aleksandr Krein, but no coverage of Veysberg (who was an associate of Gnesin and Steinberg) or Grigoriy Krein, the elder brother of Aleksandr (who studied with Gliere and knew Ippolitov-Ivanov and Khachaturyan). Unfortunate omissions.

236. Emsheimer, Ernst. "Musikethnographische Bibliographie der nichtslavischen Völker in Russland." *Acta Musicologica* 15 (1943): 34–63.

Brief introduction and list of *sigla* followed by bibliography comprising four hundred thirty-three publications, classified according to ethno-geographical influences on the music of each community. This remarkable source was compiled by a Jewish scholar in Sweden during World War II; in its ten sections, it includes non-Slavic nationalities in the Soviet Union, a rare scholarly specialty in its time period.

237. Engel, Joel. "Yevreiskaya Narodnaya Piesnya: ethnograficheskaya poyezdka letom 1912 goda." Ms., 19 typewritten pages.

Manuscript account of the ethnographic expedition of 1912 in which Ansky, Engel and others collected Jewish music (see also no. 232). Cited by Alfred Sendrey in *Bibliography of Jewish Music*, no. 2611. It does not appear to have been published in known collections of Engel's research publications.

238. Gerasimova, Julia, ed. [*Russian Periodicals and Serials*]: [*up to 1917*]. Leiden [Nether-lands]: IDC, 1998. 232, 870 microfiches and 748 microfilm reels.

Comprises 2213 periodicals dating from before the 1917 Revolution. Relevant sections for musico-cultural research include:

- Art, Theatre, Music, Cultural Life
- Jewish Periodicals

239. Ginzburg, Semen L'vovich, ed. *N.A. Rimskii-Korsakov i muzykal'noe obrazovanie: Stat'i i Materialy.* [N.A. Rimsky-Korsakov and manner of musical education: events and materials] Leningrad: Gosudarstvennoe Muzykal'noe Izdatel'stvo, 1959. 326 pp.

Biographical documentation of Andrey Nikolayevich Rimsky-Korsakov's life and work. Ginzburg, the scholar who edited this book, was a Ukrainian Jew born in Kiev in 1901 who lived through World War I, the Revolution and World War II; he died in Leningrad in 1978.

240. Glazunov, Aleksandr Konstantinovich. *Glazunov: Issledovaniia. Materialy. Publikatsii. Pis'ma.* [Research, materials, publications, writings] Otvetsvennyi Redaktor: Mark [Moisey] Osipovich Yankovskii. Leningrad: Muzgiz, 1959–1960. 2 vols.

Collection of documents related to the life and work of Aleksandr Konstantinovich Glazunov, a student of Andrey Nikolayevich Rimsky-Korsakov who later joined him on the faculty of the St. Petersburg Conservatory. Veysberg studied with both, and even when she was in Germany during 1907–1912, there was correspondence between them, which possibly influenced his participation in plans to arrange for her return to Russia.

241. Gnesin, Mikhail Fabianovich. *Mysli i Vospominaniia o N.A. Rimskom-Korsakove.* Moskva: Gos. Muzykal'noe Izdatel'stvo, 1956. 332 pp.

These reminiscences from Veysberg's fellow student and colleague include her writings and her correspondence with Glazunov, which might shed some light on her time in Germany between 1907 and 1912.

242. Golubovskii, Ivan Vasil'evich, ed. *Muzykal'nyii Leningrad 1917–1957.* Leningrad: Gosu-darstvennoe Muzykalnoe Izdatel'stvo, 1958. 526 pp.

See especially pp. 351–411, which cover the period when Veysberg and her colleagues were studying and working in St. Petersburg (including the siege of the city during World War II, which Veysberg did not survive).

243. Heskes, Irene. "Russian Nationalism and Jewish Music." *Passport to Jewish Music: Its History, Traditions, and Culture.* Milwaukee: Hal Leonard; London: Omnibus, 2002, pp. 145–51. ISBN: 9780933676459, 093367645X.

Summary history of Jewish musical nationalism in the Russian orbit covering the period from the late nineteenth century to the breakup of the Soviet Union in 1991. Includes not only composers, but also scholars and ethnomusicologists, demonstrating influence of Russian nationalism on Jews and how political changes affected the work of all. Geared toward the Yiddish-speaking communities rather than Jews in the Caucasus, the Russian Far East and Central Asia.

244. Idelsohn, Abraham Zvi. *Hebräisch-orientalischer Melodienschatz.* Jerusalem, Berlin & Wien: Benj. Harz, 1914-1929. 10 vols.

   See especially the following volumes:

   - Vol. 3 (German): *Gesänge der persischen, bucharischen und dagestanischen Juden.* li, 68 pp.
   - Vol. 3 (Hebrew): xlii, 60 pp.

245. Konchevskii, Arkadii Karlovich, ed. *Pesni Vostoka.* [Songs of the Orient] Sobrany i Zapisany v Krymu Pevtsom Etnografom A.K. Konchevskim. Garmonizovany M.A. Stavitskum i V[iach] V. Pashkalovim. Obshchaia Redaktsiia V.V. Paskhalova. Moskva: Gosudarstvennyi Institut Muzy'kalnoe Nauki, 1927. vii, 8-41 pp.

   Comprise songs from minority communities who lived in the Crimea:

   - Turetskie [Turks]
   - Palestinskie [Jews]
   - Arabskie [Arabs]
   - Privolzhskikh Tatar
   - Karaimskaia [Karaim]
   - Persidskaia [Persians]
   - Krymchatskaia [Krymchaks]

   See pages 18-25 for four Jewish songs. Also compare with no. 265, a collection of songs from the Russian Orient published a year after this group.

246. Kopytova, Galina Viktorovna & Frenkel, Aleksandr, eds. *Iz Istorii Evreiskoi Muzyki v Rossii.* [History of Jewish Music in Russia]. St. Petersburg: Evreiskii Obshchinnyi Tsentr Sankt-Peterburga-Tsentr Evreiskoi Muzyki & Rossiiskii Institut Istorii Iskusstv[o], 2006. Vol. 2. 371 pp.

   A rare book in Russian specifically devoted to music of the Jews in the former Soviet Union. Based on the proceedings of an international scientific conference "Jewish Professional Music in Russia." Publisher is devoted to Jewish historical subject matter, and Galina Viktorovna Kopytova has worked with Jascha Nemtsov on comparable projects in German, which were published in Wiesbaden and Berlin (see nos. 250-52).

247. Krebs, Stanley D. *Soviet Composers and the Development of Soviet Music.* New York: W.W. Norton, 1970. 364 pp.

   No information about Veysberg or any other female composers. The only Jewish composers among the twenty-two in the three sections of this book are Gnesin and Gliere. However, the bibliography is useful in searching for other references.

248. Moynahan, Brian. *Leningrad: Siege and Symphony.* New York: Atlantic Monthly Press, 2014. 542 pp. ISBN: 9780802123169, 0802123163.

Eyewitness written accounts of the siege of Leningrad (St. Petersburg) by the German military in 1941–1942, apposite to both ordinary inhabitants and important historical figures including Dmitri Shostakovich, who composed his *Symphony no. 7* as a musical statement of the historical events. Veysberg was among more than a million inhabitants of the city who did not survive the siege (89,968 civilians died in March 1942); while she is not specifically noted in this account, the day by day documentation of life and death in the city is more than relevant considering lack of writings from her own associates.

249. *Muzykal'nyi Sovremennik*. Periodical based in St. Petersburg (1915–1917).

Andrey Nikolayevich Rimsky-Korsakov and Veysberg, who were married, were among the editorial and authorial staff. There is a complete set of the two years this periodical was published in the Newberry Library in Chicago. See also no. 256 for related work by Marina Ovtcharenko.

250. Nemtsov, Jascha, hrsg. *Jüdische Kunstmusik im 20. Jahrhundert: Quellenlage, Entstehungsgeschichte, Stilanalysen*. Wiesbaden: [Otto] Harrassowitz, 2006. 246 pp. ISBN: 9783447052931, 3447052937.

Collection of seventeen essays, in German and English, devoted to Russian and other Eastern European Jewish composers, with a brief discussion of Jewish ethno-musicological research in the Russian orbit beginning in the early twentieth century with Ansky, Engel, Zusman Kiselgof and others.

251. Nemtsov, Jascha & Kuhn, Ernst, hrsg. *Jüdische Musik in Sowjetrussland: die "Jüdische Nationale Schule" der zwanziger Jahre*. Berlin: E[rnst] Kuhn, 2002. x, 383 pp.

252. Nemtsov, Jascha & Wehrmeyer, Andreas, hrsg. *"Samuel" Goldenberg und "Schmuyle": Jüdisches und Antisemitisches in der russischen Musikkultur. Ein internationales Symposium*. Mit Beiträgen von Marina Frolova-Walker. Mit Übersetzungen aus dem Russischen von Ernst Kuhn. Berlin: [Ernst] Kuhn, 2003. x, 302 pp. ISBN: 9783928864879, 3928864874.

Both of the above books comprise essays in German and English, which, in different ways, focus on the history of anti-Semitism and Jewish nationalism in music of the Russian Empire and the Soviet Union. *Jüdische Musik in Sowjetrussland* is based on presentations of lectures at a conference, while the fourteen essays in *"Samuel" Goldenberg und "Schmuyle"* appear to be purpose written for publication. The co-editors of these books appear to be cooperating with Russian scholars including Kopytova (see no. 246) involved in similar research.

253. *Novoye Russkoye Slovo*.

Russian newspaper based in New York City, published 1910–2010. Includes articles about music and musicians.

254. Olkhovsky, Yuri. *Vladimir Stasov and Russian National Culture*. Ann Arbor, Michigan: UMI Research Press, 1983. xii, 195 pp. ISBN: 9780835714129, 0835714128.

Based on author's PhD dissertation. ("Vladimir Stasov and His Quest for Russian National Music"), Georgetown University, 1968. 263 pp. See Chapter 6, "Stasov's Place in History," which relates his critico-historical writings to his opinion respecting nationalism among Jewish composers.

255. Ostroumova, Natalia, [ed]. *NrUSSKAQ MUZYKALXNAQ GAZETA = B [Russkaia Muzykal'-naia Gazeta*/Russian Musical Gazette, 1894–1918]. Baltimore, Maryland: RIPM International Center, 2012. 10 vols. [3, 552 pp.]

Comprises an exhaustive index of this periodical, primarily in Russian with some entries in Western European languages. The first four volumes are devoted to a chronological listing of content (events, musical works, necrology, etc.) in each weekly issue with consecutive numeration during each year. Each number is sorted by location of events. Vols. 5–10 are alphabetically arranged by keywords and author names with reference numbers apostrophizing listings in the first volumes.

256. Ovtcharenko, Marina. *Khronika Zhurnala "Muzykal'nyi Sovremennik," 1915–1917.* Baltimore, Maryland: NISC, 2004. 2 vols. [lxxi, 391 pp.] ISBNs: 9781596620001, 1596620005; 9781596620018, 1596620013; 9781596620025, 1596620021.

This is an invaluable index of all issues of the periodical *Muzykal'nyi Sovremennik* (see above), including issue numbers, the names of authors (including Veysberg) and titles. Primarily in Russian, but English/Russian introductory materials in the first volume are very helpful.

257. Pasternak, Velvel, ed. *Society for Jewish Music in St. Petersburg.* Introduction by Irene Heskes. Owings Mills, Maryland: Tara Publications, 1998. 160 pp. ISBN: 9780933676848, 0933676840.

Important data about the work of the Society (1908–1918)—especially its publications—which included collaboration from many of Veysberg's Jewish associates at the Conservatory in St. Petersburg. The Society was founded while she lived in Germany (1907–1912), but there is little doubt that she was influenced by such work after her return in 1912, although she published in other venues.

258. Pekelis, Mikhail Samoilovich. *Istoriia Russkoi Muzyki*. Moskva: Gosudarstvennoe Muzykal'noe Izdatel'stvo, 1940. 2 vols.

History of Russian music published in the first year of World War II, before research and publication of this subject matter were halted by participation in the War. Probably affected by Stalinist politics applied to music of any composers active since show trials and purges beginning in the 1930s.

Yuliya Lazarevna Veysberg 67

259. Puzyrevskii, Aleksei Il'ich & Sakketti, Liverii Antonovich. *Ocherk Piatidesiatletie deiatelnost Sankt-Peterburgskoi Konservatorii.* [Outline of the 50th Anniversary Activities of the St. Petersburg Conservatory] St. Petersburg: Tip. Glazunova, 1912. 183 pp.

    Published for the fiftieth anniversary of the St. Petersburg Conservatory, just at the time Veysberg returned there from a period in Germany (during which she studied with Max Reger and Engelbert Humperdinck), received her degree and married Andrey Nikolayevich Rimsky-Korsakov. Relevant to other students at the Conservatory as well as her.

260. Rimsky-Korsakov, Andrey Nikolayevich. *N.A. Rimskii-Korsakov: Zhizn' i Tvorchestvo.* [Nikolai Rimsky-Korsakov: Life and Works] Moskva: Ogiz Muzgiz, 1933-1946. 5 volumes in 1.

    The composer's (Nikolai Rimsky-Korsakov) son (Andrey Nikolayevich Rimsky-Korsakov, who was married to Veysberg) was responsible for the first four volumes. As the fifth volume was published after World War II (during which Andrey Nikolayevich Rimsky-Korsakov had died), it was edited by Vsevolod Andreevich Rimsky-Korsakov, Andrey Nikolayevich Rimsky-Korsakov and Veysberg's son.

261. *Rimskii-Korsakov: Issledovaniia. Materialy. Pis'ma.* [Research, Materials, Letters] Moskva: Izdatel'stvo Akademii nauk SSSR, 1953-54. 2 vols.

    Documentation of sources illustrating the life of the composer (Veysberg's teacher and father of her husband). No credited editor, in contrast to other sources attributed to the composer; his son, his grandson and his students.

262. Rimsky-Korsakov, Nikolai. *Letopis' moei Muzykal'noi Zhizni, 1844-1906.* [Chronicle of My Musical Life] St. Petersburg: M.M. Stasiulevich, 1909. v, 368 pp.

    Later editions include:

    - Leningrad: Gosudarstvennoe Izdatel'stvo, 1926. 480 pp.
    - Moskva: Gosudarstvennoe Muzykal'noe Izdatel'stvo, 1955. vii, 396 pp.
    - Moskva: Soglasie, 2004. 604 pp.

    Nikolai Rimsky-Korsakov's autobiography, which he finished shortly before his death. Complements collections of documents cited elsewhere in this section.

263. Rimsky-Korsakov, Nikolai. *Muzykal'nye stat'i i Zametki (1869-1907).* [Musical events and notices] Edited by Andrey Nikolayevich Rimsky-Korsakov [and Mikhail Fabianovich Gnesin] St. Petersburg: M.M. Stasiulevich, 1911. xlvi, 223 pp.

    Distinct from other documentary accounts of the life of Nikolai Rimsky-Korsakov in having been jointly edited by his son Andrey Nikolayevich Rimsky-Korsakov (who was married to Veysberg) and Gnesin, her fellow student and friend. Same publisher as in preceding entry—Nikolai Rimsky-Korsakov's own autobiography; presumably this was curated and edited by those close to him.

264. Sabaneev, Leonid Leonidovich. *Yevreiskaia Natsionalnaia Shkolav Muzyka.* [The Jewish National School of Music] Moskva: Obschestvo Yevreiskaya Muzyka, 1924. 31 pp. **German version**: *Die nationale jüdische Schule in der Musik.* Übersetzung von Wilhelm Tisch. Wien: Universal Edition, 1927. 24 pp. **English version**: in *Musical Quarterly* (1929), pp. 448–68.

Published as monographs in Russian and German, then translated into English for an early issue of *Musical Quarterly*, demonstrating that the essay was widely known. A prelude to Leonid Leonidovich Sabaneev's book *Modern Russian Composers* (see no. 288), which was published a few years after this essay.

265. Saminsky, Lazare. *Shest' Pesen Russkogo Vostoka.* [Six Songs of the Russian Orient] Wien: Universal Edition, 1928. 19 pp.

Collection of songs possibly influenced by field research Lazare Saminsky (who had been a student of Nikolai Rimsky-Korsakov) had done before World War I. Copy in New York Public Library. Compare with account by Arkadii Karlovich Konchevskii (no. 245).

266. Sargeant, Lynn M. *Harmony and Discord: Music and the Transformation of Russian Cultural Life.* New York: Oxford University Press, 2011. ix, 354 pp. ISBN: 9780199735266, 0199735263.

A history of Russian musical nationalism from the work of Mikhail Glinka until the Revolution. Detailed consideration of Jewish composers as an important subject in this context. In "Conclusion: Everything Old is New Again" (pp. 261–83), Veysberg is discussed in connection with her participation in the student strike at the St. Petersburg Conservatory in 1905 and her eventual return from exile in 2012, which she herself documented in *Russkaya Molva* (see no. 294 for comparison).

267. Schwartz, Boris. "Interaction Between Russian and Jewish Music and Musicians in the Nineteenth and Twentieth Centuries." *Proceedings of the World Congress on Jewish Music Jerusalem 1978.* Edited by Judith Cohen. Tel Aviv: Institute for the Translation of Hebrew Literature, Ltd., 1982, pp. 204–11. ISBN: 9789652550163, 9652550167.

No specific discussion of Veysberg, but important for unusual point of view about musical commonalities between Jewish composers from the Eastern European part of the Russian Empire and the Soviet Union. No discussion of Jewish composers from the Asian states.

268. Sidel'nikov, Viktor Mikhailovich. *Russkaia Narodnaia Pesnia: Bibliograficheskii Uzkatel' 1735–1945.* Moskva: Izdatel'stvo Akademii Nauk SSSR, 1962. 169 pp.

Bibliography of published musical writings, organized chronologically (1757–1945), and subject matter in each section classified alphabetically by name of author.

269. Slonimsky, Nicolas. *Russian and Soviet Music and Composers*. Edited by Electra Slonimsky Yourke. New York & London: Routledge, 2004. 252 pp. ISBN: 9780415968669, 0415968666.

Eyewitness accounts documenting author's personal relations with many of the greatest musicians in Russia, including details of their work. Veysberg and her husband Andrey Nikolayevich Rimsky-Korsakov are discussed on page 164.

270. Solovtsov, Anatolii Aleksandrovich. *Zhizn' i Tvorchestvo N.A. Rimskogo-Korsakova*. [Life and Creative Works of N.A. Rimsky-Korsakov] Moskva: Muzyka, 1964. 686 pp.

Biography of Nikolai Rimsky-Korsakov with assessment of his music; the most detailed and extensive such publication on the subject in the post–World War II era.

271. Tigranov, Georgiy Grigorievich, ed. *Leningradskaia Konservatoriia v Vospominaniiakh, 1862–1962*. Leningrad: Gosudarstvennoe Muzykal'noe Izdatel'stvo, 1962. 414 pp. Revised edition: Moskva: Muzyka, 1987–88. 2 vols.

Anniversary publications covering the history of the St. Petersburg Conservatory, the first on the occasion of the centennial and the second the one hundred twenty-fifth. Compare with the fiftieth anniversary book by Aleksei Il'ich Puzyrevskii and Liverii Antonovich Sakketti (no. 259).

272. Vulfius, Pavel Aleksandrovich, ed. *Iz Istorii Leningradskoi Konservatorii: Materialy i Dokumenty, 1862–1917*. Leningrad: Muzyka, 1964. 327 pp.

Another publication covering the St. Petersburg/Leningrad Conservatory. Where does this book (published in 1964, but covering only the period from the opening until the Revolution) fit in, especially since Georgiy Grigorievich Tigranov's first edition (see above) had been published only two years before this book? Possibly politically motivated.

273. Weissenberg, Dorothea. "Die Kaukasischen Bergjuden." *Mitteilungen zur jüdischen Volkskunde*. 11 (1908): 123–27, 160–71.

Two-part article in German documenting the lives of the so-called "Mountain Jews from the Caucasus," including some information about the role of music in their lives. Coincides with documentation in Russian of the ethnographic expeditions shortly before World War I in which Engel, Ansky and others participated.

274. Yankovsky, Mark [Moisey] Osipovich. *Rimskii-Korsakov i Revoliutsiia 1905 Goda*. Moskva: Muzgiz, 1950. 130 pp.

Specifically about the involvement of the faculty and students at the St. Petersburg Conservatory during the First Russian Revolution of 1905, which temporarily resulted not only in the resignation of Nikolai Rimsky-Korsakov and other faculty, but the temporary expulsion of Veysberg, Gnesin and other students.

275. Yastrebtsev, Vasilii Vasil'evich. *Moi Vospominaniia o Nikolaie Andreevichie Rimskom-Korsakovie*. Petrograd: Tip. Glavnago Upravleniia Udielov, 1917. 2 vols. **English version**: *Reminiscences of Rimsky-Korsakov*. Transl. by Florence Jonas. New York: Columbia University Press, 1985. xv, 578 pp. ISBN: 9780231052603, 023105260X.

No reference to Veysberg, but detailed discussion of her husband, Andrey Nikolayevich Rimsky-Korsakov, which provides relevant context for their marriage a few years before this book was published.

BIOGRAPHICAL

276. Bullock, Philip Ross. "Women and Music." *Women in Nineteenth-Century Russia: Lives and Culture*. Edited by Wendy Rosslyn & Alessandra Tosi. Cambridge: Open Book Publishers, 2012, pp. 119–36. ISBN: 9781906924676. 1906924678.

This account of Russian women in the long nineteenth century includes subjects from nobles to peasants, and bourgeois intellectuals who influenced education, law, medicine, music, theater, art and literature during a time most women were confined to second-class status. The period in question included the first female composers, e.g. Valentina Semenova Serova, Elena Fabianovna Gnesina and Veysberg.

277. Calvocoressi, M[ichel] D[imitri]. *A Survey of Russian Music*. Harmondworth, Middlesex, England: Penguin Books, 1944. Reprinted Westport, Connecticut: Greenwood Press, 1974. 142 pp. ISBN: 9780837168883, 0837168880.

Published in England during World War II. Most of the seventeen chapters cover important composers in chronological order, regardless of whether they were cosmopolitan or nationalist. Chapters 15–16 include introductions to Jewish and female composers whose work was barely known in English-speaking countries; Veysberg, Gnesin and Grigoriy and Aleksandr Krein are included with strong recommendations from the author.

278. Campbell, James Stuart, ed. & transl. *Russians on Russian Music, 1880–1917: An Anthology*. Cambridge [England] & New York: Cambridge University Press, 2003. 2 vols. ISBN: 9780521590976, 0521590973.

See vol. 2 for section "New Stylistic Directions" (pp. 198–233), which includes discussion of Veysberg, Gnesin and Engel.

279. Golowy, Detlef. "Veysberg, Yuliya Lazarevna." *Norton/Grove Dictionary of Women Composers*, p. 474.

Based on a short entry in the 1980 edition of *New Grove Dictionary of Music and Musicians* (vol. 19, p. 691), but far more detailed than its predecessor.

280. Haag, John. "Veysberg, Yuliya (1878–1942)." *Women in World History: A Biographical Encyclopedia*. Edited by Anne Commire & Deborah Klezmer. Waterford, Connecticut: Yorkin Publications, 1999, 2002, vol. 15, pp. 898–99. ISBN: 9780787640743, 0787640743.

Summary of Veysberg's life and career as composer and scholar, with brief citation of two references for additional information: the *New Grove* (1980 edition) and Sabaneev (see no. 288).

281. Ho, Allan & Feofanov, Dmitry, editors in chief. *Biographical Dictionary of Russian/Soviet Composers*. New York: Greenwood Press, 1989. xxv, 739 pp. ISBN: 9780313244858.

Length of this book in English outweighs many such dictionaries and encyclopedias in Russian. Each entry consists of a summary of the composer's life and a brief assessment of musical style followed by a selective list of compositions with titles and dates. References accessed by the editors are included for use of other researchers. Entry covering Veysberg is on page 574.

282. Kresten, Proteus Val Re. *Yuliya Veysberg*. Saarbrücken, [Germany]: Volut Press, 2013. 64 pp. ISBN: 9786201567313.

Based on information about Veysberg in the Wikipedia program on the Internet.

283. Loeffler, James B. *The Most Musical Nation: Jews, Culture and Nationalism in the Late Russian Empire*. New Haven, Connecticut: Yale University Press, 2010. 288 pp. ISBNs: 9780300137132, 0300137133; 9780300198300, 0300198302.

Based on the author's PhD dissertation of 2005. He deliberately limited his coverage to the period from the end of the nineteenth century to the Revolutions of 1917 and the establishment of the Soviet Union. Includes significant discussion of Jewish nationalist composers from the Conservatories in both St. Petersburg and Moscow, among whom Veysberg, Aleksandr Krein (unfortunately, however, not his brother Grigoriy Krein), Engel, Saminsky and Gnesin are noted in considerable detail.

284. Mazur, Marina Moiseevna. "Kompozitor Yuliya Veysberg: lichnostchi tvorcheskoe nasledie" (Po materialam SPB). Avtorekh dis. na soisk. uchem.k.isk. Spech 17.00.02.SPB: B.i.2002. 23 pp.

Unpublished thesis in Russian. Basis of subsequent research on Veysberg (including next entry).

285. Mazur, Marina Moiseevna. "Veysberg, Yuliya Lazarevna." *Grove Music Online* www.worldcat.org/title/veysberg-yuliya-lazarevna/oclc/5576121090&referer=brief_results. ISBN: 9781561592630.

Not to be confused with Detlef Golowy's article in *Norton/Grove Dictionary of Women Composers*. This comprises a summary of Veysberg's career as a composer, a list of prose writings she contributed to the daily newspaper *Russkaya Molva* in 1912—and literature in *Izvestiya*—as well as coverage in *Mysli Vospominaniia* of her colleague Gnesin. Note that Andrey Nikolayevich Rimsky-Korsakov was music correspondent for *Russkaya Molva* when he and Veysberg got married in 1912; the articles Veysberg contributed to this periodical are listed in the section "Scores and Editions".

286. Moisenko, Rena. "Julia Weissberg." *Realist Music: 25 Soviet Composers*. London: Meridian Books, 1949, pp. 243-48.

Significant study of the work of Veysberg; packed with information about her music beyond most other accounts of her life and work. Other composers include Gliere, Gnesin, Khachaturyan, Tikhon Khrennikov, Sergei Prokofiev, Shostakovich and Steinberg; her presence among them testifies to the respect in which her work was held.

287. Rizarev, Marina. "Weissberg (Veysberg), Juliya Lazarevna." *Encyclopedia Judaica*. Fred Skolnik, editor in chief; Michael Berenbaum, executive editor. Detroit: Macmillan/Keter Publishing House, 2007, vol. 20 [of 22], p. 737.

Inclusion of Veysberg—however briefly—in this encyclopedia demonstrates an important condition of her life, i.e. that she was Jewish by background, if not by religious practice, since she married the son of Nikolai Rimsky-Korsakov and was probably obliged to convert to Russian Orthodoxy. This was also a factor in certain other publications documenting the Jewish communities of the Russian orbit, including *Rossiiskaia Evreiskaia Entsiklopediia* and its co-project by Josif and Vitaly Charny (see no. 220).

288. Sabaneev, Leonid Leonidovich. *Modern Russian Composers*. Transl. by Judah A. Joffe. New York: International Publishers, 1927. Reprinted Freeport, New York: Books for Libraries Press, 1967. 253 pp.

Veysberg is apostrophized in the chapter "The Leningrad Group" (pp. 222-25), with other Jewish composers including Nikolai Cherepnin and Steinberg. Separate chapters on Gnesin and Aleksandr and Grigoriy Krein.

289. Taruskin, Richard. *Stravinsky and the Russian Traditions: A Biography of the Works through Mavra*. Berkeley, California: University of California Press, 1996. 2 vols. ISBNs: 9780520910379, 0520910370; 9780585366258, 058536625X.

In the chapter "The Rejoicing Discovery," Veysberg is discussed in connection with her husband Andrey Nikolayevich Rimsky-Korsakov and her brother-in-law Steinberg, and their relations with Igor Stravinsky.

290. Vodarsky-Shiraeff, Alexandria. *Russian Composers and Musicians: A Biographical Dictionary.* New York: H.W. Wilson Company, 1940. Reprinted New York: Da Capo Press, 1969. 158 pp. ISBN: 9780837125619, 0837125618.

Entry devoted to Veysberg (who was still alive when the first edition was published) is on page 140. It might also be relevant to consult the entry on her husband, Andrey Nikolayevich Rimsky-Korsakov, on pp. 108–09. While these articles are limited in length, there is information about Veysberg's compositions not found in other sources.

MUSICO-ANALYTICAL

Scores and Editions

291. Rolland, Romain. *Muzykanty Nashikh Dnei.* [Musicians of Today] Perevod s frantsrskogo Yuliya Lazarevna Veisberg. [Translated from the French by Yuliya Lazarevna Veysberg] Moskva: Muzgiz, 1938. 346 pp.

This is the most extensive of Veysberg's journalistic works, demonstrating her translational ability in multiple languages.

292. Steinberg, Maximilian. *Shest' Narodnykh Pesen. Sechs Volkslieder.* Op. 19. Wien: Universal Edition, 1931. 21 pp.

The first of four groups of folk songs in versions for orchestra and piano. Steinberg edited all four books, and Veysberg (his sister-in-law) translated the texts. This group includes the following songs:

- *Tatarskie Polon*
- *Pesnia Abdurakhmana: Bashkirskaia*
- *Dudek: Tatarskaia*
- *Tiurkskaia Liubovnaia*
- *Altai: Oiratskaia*
- *Ça ira: Frantsuaskaia Ulichnaia Pesnia Vremen Velikoi Revoliutsii*

293. Steinberg, Maximilian. *Shest' Narodnykh Pesen.* Op. 27. Wien: Universal Edition, 1932. 38 pp.

The last of four groups of folk songs in versions for orchestra and piano. Veysberg translated the texts as in the first group above. The group includes:

- *Kolykhanka: Belorusskaia*
- *Kurai: Bashkirskaia*
- *IA iz M'eresa: Ispanskaia*
- *Panenyi Solovei: Armianskaia*
- *Voznitsa iz Aviles: Ispanskaia*
- *Koza: Shutochnaia Ukrainskaia*

294. Veysberg, Yuliya Lazarevna. [Articles in *Russkaya Molva*, 1912]:
    - *"Elektra" R. Shtrausa v Marinskom Teatre*
    - *Gustav Maler*
    - *Itogi deyatel'nosti "Teatra Muzikal'noy Drami"* [Perspectives on the Activity of the "Theatre of Musical Drama"]
    - *Kontsert D. Smirnova v Pol'zu Gimnazii K. Maya v Dvoryanskom sobranii* [Smirnov's Concert in Support of K. May's Gymnasium in the Noble Assembly]
    - *Perviy Russkiy Simfonicheskiy Kontsert* [The First Russian Symphonic Concert]
    - *203 Simfonicheskiy Kontsert Grafa Sheremeteva* [The 203rd Symphonic Concert of Count Sheremetev]
    - *Vagner i Zhenschini* [Wagner and Women]

    See no. 266 for relevant contextual observations from Sargeant regarding contributions to this periodical.

295. Veysberg, Yuliya Lazarevna. *Romansy*. Op. 1. Leipzig: M.P. Belaiev, 1911. Reprinted as *Drei Lieder*. Huntsville, Texas: Recital Publications, 1994. 17 pp.

    Comprises three songs for voice and piano in Russian with German translations:
    - *Piesnia: Oi Poshlab ia zhit' na volie/Lied: Hei wie wollt' so frei ich streifen*
    - *Vykhozhu odin ia na dorogu/Einsam geh' ich fern vom Stadtgewimmer*
    - *Zhizn' eshcheperedo mnoiu/Leben liegt noch leuchtend vor mir*

296. Veysberg, Yuliya Lazarevna. *Deux Chansons pour Chant et Piano*. Op. 2. Leipzig: M.P.

    The two songs are based on texts of Paul Verlaine, with the original texts and translations in Russian and German:
    - *Le ciel est au dessus le toit/Kak nebo nad kroblei tam/Der Himmel ruht dort überm Dach*
    - *Chanson d'automne: "Les sanglots longs"/Osseniaia piesn': "Kak skripok ston"/Herbstlied: "So schluchzend bang"*

297. Veysberg, Yuliya Lazarevna. *Rautendelein: Tri Pi'sni dliya soprano s orkestrom*. Op. 3. Leipzig: M.P. Belaiev, 1912. Reprinted Huntsville, Texas: Recital Publications, 1994. 16 pp.

    Piano-vocal arrangement of the orchestral original. All texts are from *Die versunkene Glocke* of Gerhard Hauptmann. They comprise three songs in German, Russian and English:
    - *Ne znaiu, kto otkuda ia/Weiss nicht woher ich kommen bin*
    - *Kuda? Kuda? shel pir goroi/Wohin? Wohin? Ich sass beim Mahl*
    - *IA kosy svoi pletu pri lunie/Im hellen Monde kämm' mein Haar*

298. Veysberg, Yuliya Lazarevna. *Noch'iu: Simfoniches'kaia Kartina/In der Nacht.* Op. 10. Poem by F. Tyutchev. German transl. by Ellinor Johannsen. Wien: Universal Edition, 1929. 31 pp. [See also *Nachts: Simfonisches Gedicht für Orchester* published Hamburg: Sikorski, n.d.]

Orchestral tone poem, the scoring of which comprises three flutes/piccolo, two oboes/English horn, two clarinets/bass clarinet, two bassoons/contrabassoon, four horns, three trumpets, three trombones and tuba.

299. Veysberg, Yuliya Lazarevna. *Ballada dlia bol'shogo Orkestra.* Op. 12. Moskva: Universal'noe Izdatel'stvo; Wien: Universal Edition, 1930. 55 pp.

Based on a poem of Heinrich Heine about Harald Harfagar. The scoring of this work comprises two flutes/piccolo, two oboes/English horn, two clarinets/bass clarinet, two bassoons/contrabassoon, four horns, three trumpets, three trombones, tuba, timpani, percussion, harp and strings.

300. Veysberg, Yuliya Lazarevna. *Skazočka dlia Orkestra/Ein Märchen (Fingerhütchen) fuer Orchester.* Op. 13. Moskva: Muzsektor Gosizdata; Wien: Universal Edition, 1928. 59 pp. [See also *Ein Märchen nach dem Gedicht "Der kleine Fingerhut" von Ferdinand Mayer* published Hamburg: Sikorski, n.d., and described as "instrumental chamber music."]

Orchestral tone poem. The original orchestration in the score published in 1928 comprises two flutes/piccolo, two oboes/English horn, three clarinets, two bassoons, four horns, two trumpets, three trombones, tuba, timpani, two percussion (unspecified), celesta, two harps and strings.

301. Veysberg, Yuliya Lazarevna. *Gusi-Lebedi: Detskaia Opera v Chetyrekh Epizodikh.* [Geese-Swans] Op. 18. Leningrad: Gosudarstvennoe Izdatel'stvo "Iskusstvo," 1938. Reprinted Moskva: Muzgiz, 1960. 70 pp. **English version**: *The Wild Geese. Soviet Opera for Children.* Transl. by John Alford. London: The Workers' Music Association, 1942. 64 pp.

This opera for children was based on a libretto by Samuil Yakovlevich Marshak, a Russian Jewish poet. The work was dedicated to Evgenia Fabianovna Gnesina, one of the sisters of Gnesin involved in the Gnesin Music Institute.

302. Veysberg, Yuliya Lazarevna. *Pyat' Detskikh Pesen [Detskiia Pesni].* [Five Songs of Children] Op. 23. Moskva: Muzikal'nii Sektor Gosudarstvennoe Izdatel'stvo, 1929. 13 pp.

Comprises the following songs for voice and piano:

- *Babochka/Schmetterling*
- *Zain'ka/Häschen*
- *Mishi/Mäuslein*
- *Loshad'/Pferdchen*
- *Korabaik/Schifflein*

303. Veysberg, Yuliya Lazarevna. *Iz Persidskoi Lirik/Aus dem Persischen Lyrik*. Op. 26. Dlia golosa s fortepiano. Moskva: Muzsektor Gosizdata; New York & Wien: Universal Edition, [1926]. 7 pp.

Two texts translated from the poetry of Omar Khayyam:

- *Kniga Iunosti/Buch der Jugend*
- *IA voz'mu bokal/Auf der Lippen schäumt der Becher*

304. Veysberg, Yuliya Lazarevna. *Shest' Moldavskikh Pesen [Moldavskie Pesni], dlia golosa s Fortepiano.* Op. 55. Tekst Narodn'ii Perevod A. Borsh, Yu. Veisberg i E. Lebedevoii. Leningrad: Gosudarstvennoe Muzikal'noe Izdatel'stvo, 1941. 21 pp.

Comprises six Moldavian songs for voice and piano:

- *Tam, v teni*
- *Listokhek Vinograda*
- *Chaban (Pastukh)*
- *Gor'kaia Toska*
- *Kukushka*
- *Ilyana*

305. Veysberg, Yuliya Lazarevna. *Lunnaia Skazka/Mondmärchen [Wiegenlied].* Für eine Singstimme, Flöte, Harfe und Streichquartett. Moscou: Section Musicale des Editions d'Etat, 1929. 13 pp.

A rare work of chamber music from this composer. Unusual scoring.

306. Veysberg, Yuliya Lazarevna. *Pesnia Giul'nary iz Opery "Giul'nara": dlia Vysokogo golosa s f[orte]-p[iano].* Moskva: Gosudarstvennoe Muzykal'noe Izdatel'stvo RSFSR, 1935. 9 pp.

Aria from the opera *Giul'nara* (1935).

307. Veysberg, Yuliya Lazarevna. *Matrosskaia Pliaska/Danse des Matelots.* Moskva: Ogiz Muzgiz, 1936. 31 pp.

Originally composed in 1926. From the opera *Rusalochka* [The Little Mermaid], based on Hans Christian Andersen.

Index

Abdul-Rahim, Raoul 126
Absher, Amy 127
Akulova, L.V. 231
Alford, John 301
Alvarez, Leticia 192
Ammer, Christine 19
An Pyŏng-uk 40
Andersen, Hans Christian 307
Angles, Higinio 178
Ansky, Shlomo [*pseudonym*
  of Shmuel Rapaport] 232
Arthur, Donald 55
Ashton, E.B. 66
Axmann, David 84

Bacher, Wilhelm 233
Bailey, Brooke 12
Baneva, Evelina 87
Baqueiro Fóster, Geronimo 182
Barce, Ramón 193
Bassa, Il'i 58
Bat-Adah, Hagit 91
Bayer, Bathja 234
Beaumont, Antony 65
Bell, Mufrida 111
Benincasa, Carmine 59
Berenbaum, Michael 287
Berg, Alban 74, 83
Berger, Hilde 41
Bernandt, Grigorii Borisovich 219
Blakesly, Melissa 156
Blaukopf, Herta 42
Block, Adrienne Fried 1
Boelza, Igor F. 235
Bonds, Margaret 128
Borsh, A. 304
Boucher, Agnès 43, 44
Bowers, Jane 20
Boyd, Melinda 9
Branover, Herman 220
Braun, Sevgi 8
Brinker-Gabler, Gisela 63

Briscoe, James R. 27, 28, 29, 105, 156
Britt, David 59
Brown, Elsa Barkley 141
Brown, Rae Linda 117, 119, 129, 130, 131,
  142, 143, 144, 163, 165, 166, 168
Brusatti, Otto 34
Buchheister, Cristina 57
Buchmayr, Friedrich 45
Bullock, Philip Ross 276

Calvocoressi, M[ikhail] D[imitry] 277
Campbell, James Stuart 278
Campos Fonseca, Susan 194
Carbone, María Teresa 57
Carredano, Consuelo 173
Casares Rodicio, Emilio 174, 195, 196
Charny, Josif 220
Charny, Vitaly 220
Chase, Gilbert 175
Chiti, Patricia Adkins 21
Citron, Marcia J. 46
Claessens, Peter 65
Claghorn, Charles E. 2
Cohen, Aaron 3
Cohen, Judith 267
Colerus, Blanca 47
Commire, Anne 280
Cook, Susan C. 22
Creighton, Basil 67

Deane, Raymond 60
DeLerma, Dominique Rene 118
Desmond, William 70
Dimoski, Sašo 48
Dohi, Yoshio 57
Dolzhanskiĭ, Aleksandr Naumovich 219
Draayer, Suzanne Rhodes 177
Dubnow, Simon 225
Dykema, Dan 133

Ebel, Otto 13
Edwards, J. Michele 26

77

Elliott, Fiona 86
Emsheimer, Ernst 236
Engel, Yoel (Joel) 228, 237
Escal, Françoise 49

Fabre, Geneviève 142
Famera, Karen 18
Farrah, Scott David 144
Feith, Michel 142
Feldman, Walter Zev 222
Feofanov, Dmitry 281
Fernández de la Cuesta, Ismael 174
Filler, Susan M. 30, 92, 105, 110, 113
Floyd, Samuel A., Jr. 119, 120, 130
Follet, Diane 93
Franklin, Peter 50
Frenkel, Aleksandr 246
Freytag, Veronika 33
Frigyesi, Judit 222
Frolova-Walker, Marina
Fry, Varian 35
Fuller, Sophie 134

Gaillard-Paquet, J.M. 57
Gallwitz, Klaus 51
Galván, Gary 180
Garcia Vila, Antonio 52
Geralds, Marion 94
Gerasimova, Julia 238
Ginzburg, Semen L'vovich 239
Giroud, Francoise 53
Giustinelli, Luisella Cassetta 54
Glazunov, Aleksandr Konstantinovich 240
Glickman, Sylvia 23, 113
Gnesin, Mikhail Fabianovich 241, 263
Godoy, Susan 183
Golowy, Detlef 279
Golubovskiĭ, Ivan Vasil'evich 242
González Peña, Maria Luz 174
Gray, Anne 4
Green, Mildred Denby 135, 136
Greeson, James 137
Grönke, Kadja 95
Guigui-Stollberg, Jacqueline 86
Guler, Suna 70
Günzberg, David 225
Guseva, Ju. 87

Haag, John 280
Haas, Willy 66
Haake, Chas. J. 160, 161
Haake, Gail Martin 160, 161
Haces, Luis Romano 58, 66
Hague, Eleanor 184
Harkavy, Albert 225
Hauptmann, Gerhard 297
Heard, Richard 164
Heine, Heinrich 299
Helguera, Luis Ignacio 189
Hennessee, Don A. 5
Herrberg, Heike 36
Heskes, Irene 243, 257
Hilmes, Oliver 55
Hine, Darlene Clark 141
Hixon, Don L. 5
Ho, Allan 281
Hofmeister, Friedrich 221
Holzer, Linda Ruth 146
Høybye, Eva 91
Hughes, Langston 170
Hundert, Gershon David 222

Iampolskiĭ, Izrail Markovich 226
Iankovskiĭ, Mark [Moisey] Osipovich 240, 274
Iastrebtsev, Vasiliĭ Vasil'evich 275
Idelsohn, Abraham Zvi 244
Igou, Orrin Lincoln 185
Il'inskii, Aleksandr Aleksandrovich 223
Isaacs, Reginald 56

Jackson, Barbara Garvey 131, 138, 162, 165
Jacobshagen, Arnold 94
Jacobson, Marion 222
Jaffé, Daniel 224
Jezic, Diane Peacock 24
Joffe, Judah A. 288
Johannsen, Ellinor 298
Johnson, Calvert 158
Jonas, Florence 275

Kandinsky, Nina 57
Kaplan, Gilbert 114, 115
Katzenelson, Judah Leib Benjamin 225
Kazmier, Will 147
Keckhauer, Mike 133

Index

Keegan, Susanne 58
Keldysh, Iurii Vsevolodovich 226
Kenny, Aisling 95
Khayyam, Omar 303
Kibbe, Michael 167
Kimball, Carol 106
Klarmann, Adolf D. 88
Klezmer, Deborah 280
Kokoschka, Oskar 59
Konchevskii, A[rkadii] K[arlovich] 245
Kopytova, Galina Viktorovna 246
Kostick, Gavin 60
Koves, Peter 61
Kravitt, Edward F. 96
Krebs, Stanley D. 247
Kresten, Proteus Val Re 282
Krüger, Werner 57
Kuhn, Ernst 251, 252

La Grange, Henry-Louis de 67
Lasseter, Leslie 26
Lazarova, Diana 66
Lebedevoĭ, E. 304
Lee, Ellen 62
Leidzen, Erik W.G. 169
Levin, Neil
Lewisohn, Ludwig 89
Loeffler, James B. 222, 283
López-Calo, José 174
Lynch, Janet Nichols 139
Lynn, Jennifer Kaye 197

Mahler, Gustav 114, 115
Mahler-Werfel, Alma Maria
  Schindler 63, 64, 65, 66, 67, 84,
  105, 106, 107, 108, 109, 110, 111,
  112, 113, 114, 115, 116
Mahony, Patrick 97
Mann, Stephan 51
Marchegay, Gilberte 66
Marco, Tomás 186
Margarit, Isabel 68
Marshak, Samuil Yakovlevich 301
Martner, Knud 98
Matthews, Colin 112
Matthews, David 112
Mayer, Clara 6
Mayer, Ferdinand 300

Mayer-Serra, Otto 187
Mazur, Marina Moiseevna 284, 285
McConathy, Osbourne 160, 161
McVicker, Mary F. 25
Meerwein, Georg G. 56
Mendoza, Vicente T. 188
Mitchell, Donald 67
Modigliani, Denise 79
Moham, Carren D. 140
Moisenko, Rena 286
Monahan, Seth 69
Monson, Karen 70
Montero, Rosa 71
Moreno-Rivas, Yolanda 189
Morris, Mellasenah 141
Moynahan, Brian 248
Muller, Lise Lotte 37

Nachman, Myrna 131
Nemec, Claudia 72
Nemtsov, Jascha 250, 251, 252
Netzer, Remigius 59
Neuls-Bates, Carol 1, 14
Nyaho, William Chapman 159

Olivier, Antje 7, 8, 15
Olkhovsky, Yuri 254
Öney, Gulnar 57
Ono, Setsuko 91
Ostroumova, Nataliĭa 255
Ovtcharenko, Marina 256

Pashkalov, Viach 245
Pasternak, Velvel 257
Patterson, Lindsay 128
Pedersen, Gunner 53
Peebles, Sarah Louise 148
Peham, Helga 73
Pekelis, Mikhail Samoĭlovich 258
Pena, Joaquín 178
Pendle, Karin 9, 26, 46
Perle, George 74
Petala, Manōlē 91
Phelps, Shirelle
Phillips, Max 75
Price, Florence Beatrice (Smith) 132, 156,
  157, 158, 159, 160, 161, 162, 163, 164,
  165, 166, 167, 168, 169, 170, 171, 172

Prieto [Fernández de la Llana], María
  Teresa 199, 201, 202, 203, 204, 205, 206,
  207, 208, 209, 210, 211, 212, 213, 214,
  215, 216, 217, 218
Pulido, Esperanza 190, 191, 200
Puzyrevskiĭ, Aleksei Il'ich 259

Querol, Miguel 178

Rapaport, Shmuel see Ansky, Shlomo
Reich, Nancy 10
Reisser, Marsha J. 120, 121
Ricart Matas, José 179
Rieger, Eva 63, 116
Riemann, Hugo 228
Rieschel, Hans-Peter 76
Rietenauer, Erich 77
Rimskiĭ-Korsakov, Andrei Nikolaevich
  249, 260, 263
Rimskiĭ-Korsakov, Nikolai Andreevich 261,
  262, 263
Rimskiĭ-Korsakov, Vsevolod Andreevich 260
Ring, Montague 172
Rizarev, Marina 287
Rode-Breymann, Susanne 65, 78, 99
Rognoni, Luigi 67
Rolland, Romain 291
Rosslyn, Wendy 276
Roster, Danielle 79
Rothkamm, Jörg 100
Rousseau-Dujardin, Jacqueline 49

Sabaneev, Leonid Leonidovich 264, 288
Sabaté, Hernan 70
Sadie, Julie Anne 16
Sakketti, Liverii Antonovich 259
Saminsky, Lazare 265
Samuel, Rhian 16
Santana, Juan 198
Sargeant, Lynn M. 266
Sauvat, Catherine 80
Sawyer, Lisa Lee 149
Schäfer, Ursel 53
Schleifer, Martha Furman 23, 113, 165, 180
Schoenberg, Arnold 64
Schollum, Robert 101
Schwartz, Boris 267
Sebestyen, Gyorgy 47
Seele, Astrid 81

Sendrey, Alfred [Aladár Alfred Szendrei] 229
Shanzer, Andrea 59
Shelton, Teresa Lorraine 150
Shirley, Wayne 168
Shteinpress, Boris Solomonovich 226
Shteynberg, Maksimilyan Oseevich 292, 293
Sidel'nikov, Viktor Mikhailovich 268
Sine, Nadine 113
Skolnik, Fred 287
Skowronski, Jo Ann 122, 123
Slobin, Mark 222
Slonimsky, Nicolas 269
Smith, Bethany Jo 151
Smith, Jessie Carney 124
Smith, Warren Storey 102
Solovtsov, Anatoliĭ Aleksandrovich 270
Sordo Sodi, Carmen 201
Sorell, Walter 82
Soroker, Iakov L'vovich 230
Southern, Eileen 125, 152
Spielmann, Heinz 37
Spiess, Lincoln Bunce 181
Stadtlander, Karen 90
Stavitskii, M.A. 245
Steiger, Martina 83
Stern, Susan 11
Still, William Grant 157, 167
Stock, R.M. 53
Suarez, César 91
Světlik, Eduard 87
Swierenga, Aleid 82

Tabe, Shukuko 57
Taruskin, Richard 289
Tautou, Alexis 65
Taylor, Vivian 171
Tekorius, Alfonsas 87
Temes, Jose Luis 210
Tenner, Haide 64
Terborg-Penn, Rosalyn 141
Tick, Judith 20
Tigranov, Georgiy Grigorievich 271
Tisch, Wilhelm 264
Tischler, Alice 153
Tomasic, Carol 153
Tomlinson-Brown, Rebecca Hanna 103
Toorn, Willem van 66
Torberg, Friedrich 84
Torberg, Marietta 84

Index

Tosi, Alessandra 276
Tsou, Judy S. 22
Tyutchev, Feodor 298

Urban, Juliane 104

Vayon, Pablo J. 202
Veidlinger, Jeffrey 222
Vergo, Peter 38
Verlaine, Paul 296
Veysberg, Yuliya Lazarevna [Weissberg/ Veisberg, Iuliïa/Julia/Julie] 249, 291, 292, 293, 294, 295, 296, 297, 298, 299, 300, 301, 302, 303, 304, 305, 306, 307
Vodarsky-Shiraeff, Alexandria 290
Vondenhoff, Bruno 31, 32, 33
Vondenhoff, Eleonore 31, 32, 33
Vulfius, Pavel Aleksandrovich 272

Wagner, Heidi 36
Walker-Hill, Helen 172
Walter, Käte 116
Walton, Christopher 85
Wehrmeyer, Andreas 252
Weidinger, Alfred 86
Weingartz-Perschel, Karin 7, 15
Weissenberg, Dorothea 273
Weissensteiner, Friedrich 87
Weissweiller, Eva 17
Welky, Ali 133
Werfel, Franz 88, 89
Werup, Marie 91
Wessling, Berndt W. 90
White, Stephanie Lawrence 154
Wollenberg, Susan 95
Wright-Pryor, Barbara 155

Xenakis, Françoise 91

Yampolskiï, *see* Iampolskiï, Izrail Markovich
Yankovskiï, *see* Iankovskiï, Mark [Moisey] Osipovich
Yastrebtsev, *see* Iastrebtsev, Vasiliï Vasil'evich
Yourke, Electra Slonimsky 269

Zahn, Leopold 39
Zaimont, Judith Lang, 18 191
Zeschitz, Renate 70
Zhang Xiuya 89

Printed in the United States
by Baker & Taylor Publisher Services